The Bible Belt Mystique

The Bible Belt Mystique

By
C. DWIGHT DOROUGH

THE WESTMINSTER PRESS
Philadelphia

Book Design by Dorothy Alden Smith

Published by The Westminster Press®
Philadelphia, Pennsylvania

PRINTED IN THE UNITED STATES OF AMERICA

Grateful acknowledgment is given for permission to use
the following:

An excerpt from "The Hills of Zion." Copyright 1926
by Alfred A. Knopf, Inc., and renewed 1954 by H. L.
Mencken. Reprinted from *A Mencken Chrestomathy*,
by H. L. Mencken, by permission of the publisher.

Excerpts from *Miracle Magazine*. Reprinted by permission of Don Stewart Evangelistic Association,
Phoenix, Arizona.

Library of Congress Cataloging in Publication Data

Dorough, C. Dwight, 1912–
  The Bible belt mystique.

  Includes bibliographic references.
  1. Southern States—Religion.   I. Title.
BR535.D67   269'.2'0975   74-11395
ISBN 0-664-20709-X

To
Ivy Anderson Dorough

Contents

An Aside to the Reader

ALTHOUGH MUCH of my material comes from libraries, I have been told that personal experiences are evident. Reared in an atmosphere of religion and politics by Southern parents and grandparents, I observed at close range in my childhood the twentieth-century version of my subject. My first experience with brush arbors, spirited singing, box suppers, dinners on the ground, and hellfire preaching I cannot date, for these were familiar in the culture of northeastern Texas long before I was born. I am tempted to write a book that deals primarily in reminiscences, but I seriously doubt that I could contribute anything to the subject that thousands of people of my generation and background have not shared. My plan in this book is to concentrate on the historical backgrounds (the late eighteenth and first half of the nineteenth century) and then to observe some of the twentieth-century survivals. Since some of the material, on camp meetings, for example, has been presented by scholars to more academic audiences, I want to address myself primarily to the layman. My principal purpose is merely to describe the older faith and to single out some of the recent examples with which I am familiar.

Indeed personal experience does enter into an interpretation of materials like these. At times I have felt

like a participant in these early manifestations of religiousness. I hope that those readers born in the early
years of this century will share the same sort of identity
as they recall the many little incidents that resemble
those in their own lives or in those of their antebellum
forebears. I shall share a few reminiscent notes, illustrative of the personal element, which will indicate that I
am attuned to the subject. I was about four years of age
when I heard for the first time the shrill voice of a
woman crying out in the "unknown tongue" at an open-
air church service. With both hands extended in a quivering fashion over her head and a look of hysteria, she
appeared to me in a miserable state of mind, but a moment later she fell to the ground in exhausted bliss.
When I was ten an itinerant Pentecostal preacher
stopped off at my paternal grandparents' house and was
invited to stay for the midday meal. Before we assembled at the table, he asked us to get down on our
knees so that he could pray. This man had a peculiar
style; he turned the straight chair around and pulled
the back firmly up against the top of his head. He de-
voted much of his loud eloquence to me in great concern for the status of my sinful soul. I wondered at the
time what it was all about, not being able to think of
anything bad I had done, certainly nothing he could
have known about on such a short acquaintance. Besides, boys were told in those days that they had a certain immunity until they were twelve years of age, and
I still had two years of theoretical freedom until I
would be held accountable for my actions. However, a
few years later, after a presiding elder (now called a
district superintendent) of the Methodist church paid a
similar tribute to me, I may have discovered the secret.
I was being recruited for the ministry. But if this were
the case, why did these men not look around for someone who would need less spiritual rehabilitation? But
maybe all young people were wicked in those days.

Had no one heard of Emerson and the Unitarians, with all their emphasis on the divinity of man? Even if a preacher had heard about these "heretics," he would not have referred to them among decent folk.

Speaking of prayers before a meal, I cannot refrain from telling about a near-disaster. A great-uncle of mine in Oklahoma called on a Baptist preacher to ask the blessing and the man proceeded to deliver a sermon. My great-aunt had removed all the food from the oven and had placed it in the warming compartment above the wood cookstove. Realizing she had failed to put the cornbread in the oven, she quickly did so before we all sat down at the table, and my uncle called on the good brother to pray. Time was no consideration to these gentlemen, certainly not to the Baptist, Methodist, Nazarene, and Pentecostal brethren I recall. However, the Presbyterian ministers, who received their invitations from my mother's side of the house, seemed to be of a more practical bent on these occasions, for they knew that few souls could be saved on an empty stomach. They made their prayers brief, and we got on with the business of the moment. But this Baptist preacher was of a different type. With eyes closed and head nodding up and down in a regular rhythm, he paid tribute to all of God's handiwork here on earth and then he zeroed in on the beautiful hills surrounding the farmhouse where we were at the moment. At this point I discovered the cause of my aunt's nervousness and kicking of her husband's shins. I could smell bread burning. Then suddenly I caught a glimpse of my uncle crawling along the floor behind the table, then down the other side of the dining room and into the kitchen across the squeaking floor to the stove, where he opened the oven door and pulled the bread out, then began the long crawl back to his seat on the opposite side of the dining room. When he rounded the table and entered the backstretch, the reverend brother said, "And now, Lord,

bless this home," but when he began mentioning everyone sitting there individually, I knew that my uncle
would make it back without being discovered in his
act of irreligiousness.

The summer revival meetings in my hometown of
Bonham, Texas, were always a time of brisk activity, a
welcomed relief from the small-town routine when there
was little to look forward to except the county fair and
football season, still two months away. The "white pri-
maries" were over and the runoffs had settled the political picture, since there were only about eleven registered Republicans in all of Fannin County (this was
Sam Rayburn country). But the outdoor services that
left the most indelible impression on me were the ones
attended with my grandparents, at the rural camp meeting sites. I remember the fragrance of fresh straw upon
which the children's quilts were spread, and I have
often felt sorry for the little folks who came along a bit
later when sawdust replaced the straw, because grown-
ups under duress kicked up considerable dust in the
struggle to shed their sins and get saved. An account of
a meeting at one of the small-town churches will appear
in the latter part of the book.

Withholding prejudice and concealing denominational identity might appear difficult in a book like this.
Having done my formal research over a period of thirty
years, I suppose I have mellowed a bit and have come
to accept even the most sensational expression as a part
of the human effort. I have also come to realize that
religion does not necessarily produce a behavior entirely complimentary to the Christians in my society.
Certainly a professor who has taught a course in Southern literature for thirty years can only be grateful for
having such a varied background in a regional culture.
My research in Southern politics, participation in cam-
paigns, holding of a position for several years in the attorney general's office, and, finally, writing of the biog-

raphy of the late Speaker of the House of Representatives Sam Rayburn (for Random House) have all added to my experience in the human drama. A retired Methodist minister chanced to read an earlier draft of the present manuscript and wrote an unsolicited appraisal which made me feel that I had achieved some degree of objectivity. "It reads," he said, "just page after page, like things I heard in my childhood and upbringing in Martin, northwest Tennessee. I have come to wonder where you grew up. I know you got lots of it out of books but the personal equation, while mild, is persistent. But to this good hour I have not decided to what faith you adhere, tho' I have a faint surmise you lean a bit toward the Methodist."

Since this book is primarily for the layman, not for the church historian, I have been selective and have used a type of documentation that could prove annoying to that sort of critic or scholar who is more concerned with what has been left out than with what has been put in, and reads the notes first. The sections about camp meetings are based upon some of my doctoral research and lectures in Southern literature, updated periodically. Here I have been concerned more with the origins of this earlier religiousness and, in the interest of brevity, and the elimination of repetition, as well as in preference for more typically Southern subjects, I have necessarily passed over figures such as Charles Finney, Gipsy Smith, Sam Jones, Dwight L. Moody (for whom I was named), George Stuart, and Billy Sunday— all of a later period. Books like William G. McLoughlin, Jr.'s *Modern Revivalism: Charles Grandison Finney to Billy Graham* and Bernard A. Weisberger's *They Gathered at the River* will serve those who insist upon some things I have elected to omit, or who prefer a different approach. My purpose is to give a historical perspective of the Bible Belt mystique in its formative years and to point out certain twentieth-century manifestations and effects that I have observed.

A portion of the material on camp meetings was given as a lecture before the Torch Club of Houston and was later published in the club's journal ("The Old Time Religion: Camp Meetings in the South," *The Torch,* Vol. XXXII, October 1959, pp. 16–23). It is used here by permission of *The Torch.*

A few readers will possibly find some ideas lying between the lines that through sensitivity, defensiveness, or pious arrogance they might attribute to me. I am well aware that a book on Southern religion can lead an author into much unwelcomed controversy. Benjamin Franklin once gave some good advice to a friend who sent him a manuscript on reason and religion for his comment before publication: ". . . the consequence of printing this piece will be a great deal of odium drawn upon yourself, mischief to you, and no benefit to others. He that spits against the wind, spits in his own face. . . . I should advise you, therefore, not to attempt unchaining the tiger, but to burn this piece before it is seen by any other person; whereby you will save yourself a great deal of mortification from the enemies it may raise against you, and perhaps a good deal of regret and repentance." [1] But the presence of this book before you proves, perhaps, that "advice is least heeded when most needed."

C.D.D.

1

The Nature
of the Old-Time Religion

WHEN H. L. MENCKEN of the *American Mercury* referred to a particular type of conservative religion as
belonging to the "Bible Belt," he left the impression
that he referred to a special geographical section, perhaps the equivalent of the corn belt, cotton belt, or cit-
rus fruit belt. What he meant was that rural section of
the South whose populace was composed of pious folk
who expressed their type of religiousness by earnest
praying, hymn singing, Bible study, and proselyting. In
the twentieth century many of the exponents of this
type of fundamentalism have been referred to as "the
unsuccessful middle class." William G. McLoughlin,
Jr., in his *Modern Revivalism,* explains that many of
these had been tenant farmers and poor whites who had
migrated to the larger cities to find work in industry
when their rural economy failed to supply their needs.
Here they attempted to re-create the type of religious
atmosphere they had enjoyed in the country; hence,
tabernacles and tents became familiar sights in the
crowded residential areas where such people lived.[1] To
some the "Bible Belt" is really a term that reflects an attitude, a type of conservatism that is not confined to any
special section of America. It might apply to the city as
well as to the country. The term has even been used by
those who would cast aspersion on a faith that they find

objectionable because of its anti-intellectual origin, conservatism, and apparent obsolescence. Since the concept is somewhat ambiguous it might appear inappropriate. Its nebulous nature, however, does not destroy its connotative power, for it is highly suggestive of an approach to religion that does not have to be relegated to any particular economic or social class, but for the purpose of this book it will be confined geographically to the South. Also this book will deal heavily in background and sources, that is, with the emphasis upon the formative years of the late eighteenth and early nineteenth centuries, describing the origins of the old-time religion. The last four chapters will show some of the twentieth-century expressions of the Bible Belt mystique.

Auguste Comte states that thought goes through three stages: the theological, the metaphysical, and the scientific. Religion, he says, emerges in the first, modulates into philosophy in the second, and disappears in the third. In the broadest sense, the religious thought of the Old South was primarily theological, but when it was conveyed to a frontier people by circuit and farmer preachers it lost much of its intellectual and rational quality. While it preserved these more academic characteristics in the settled communities among Episcopalian and Presbyterian ministers, it often degenerated into emotionalism and primitivism in the sparsely settled regions, most frequently among those of Methodist and Baptist persuasion.

Actually there are two sides to this religion—the empirical (or emotional) and the rational. The first half has been loosely referred to as the "old-time religion" or the "faith of our fathers." It involves revivalism and the camp meeting with all the attendant strange behavior, and it involves the missionary in homespun who carried the gospel to a people hungering for spiritual sustenance. It pertains also to the Negro slave with his

peculiar type of piety that has made him an inseparable
member of Southern society, but a study of black religion will not be included in this volume.

The second side of Southern religion—the rational—
would necessarily involve a consideration of the cardinal doctrines of the Reformation and the numerous
creeds that evolved from them, as well as of the conflicts over theology and dogma, and of the orthodox reaction to liberalism and heterodoxy. Because of the
complexity of these subjects, the more rational treatment of them has been passed over rather sketchily;
however, the author of these pages examined these
areas in his Ph.D. dissertation at the University of
Texas, August 1944 (directed by Dr. Theodore Horn-
berger). Hence the present book will deal with what
may appear to be the more sensational features of
Southern religion, but the faith that evolved from such
extravagance is by far the most significant. It helped
produce a religious and political solidarity that contributed to the Bible Belt mystique.

However, this type of religiousness served a purpose,
in spite of the rowdyism, controversies, and anti-intellectual biases. It tamed a frontier people and helped
to restore some degree of order in the more lawless sections. It gave direction to a multitude of derelict souls
and supported the new frontier democracy. For some it
may have proved only a sedative or a narcotic, with all
the weaknesses of a faith that puts salvation into mass
production.

The present-day South has felt the full impact of this
enigma. The Southern part of the United States has
prided itself in its religiousness, but since the Civil War
it has been plagued by problems for which one might
assume Christianity would provide some guidance.
While the intent of this book is neither to engage in
caustic indictment nor to offer solutions, recognition
must be given to the role that the old-time religion has

played in maintaining a type of *status quo* that many scholars regard as typically Southern. In the area of race relations the South's problems—not necessarily confined to the South—have become increasingly complex during the twentieth century.

In a comprehensive volume entitled *The Authoritarian Personality,* one of the conclusions reached is as follows: "Belonging to or identifying oneself with a religious body in America today certainly does not mean that one thereby takes over the traditional Christian values of tolerance, brotherhood, and equality." [2] Actually the people who do not affiliate with the churches are the champions of such values. Then one might add that social attitudes are not influenced by affiliation with one of the large religious groups. As a rule, the majority join a church today not so much because of a theological or ideological commitment but more for very practical or mundane reasons—for status, for its youth program, its recreational facilities, its physical plant, its professional staff, or its proximity to the home. People are drawn together by similar interests. As in the nineteenth century, they adapt an emotionalism to fit their immediate needs and find in it a rationalization for their attitudes and behavior. [3]

Samuel A. Stouffer's *Communism, Conformity, and Civil Liberties* suggests that the problems of the South in this respect are more acute than are those in other parts of the country. Stouffer shows that the South's greater intolerance may result from an educational factor. He also points out that churchgoers are more intolerant of nonconformists than are nonchurchgoers. [4] Unchristian attitudes are incubated in a so-called Christian environment.

H. Shelton Smith's *In His Image, but . . . Racism in Southern Religion, 1780–1910* has pursued this line of thought. He traces the history of racism in Southern religion, supporting the thesis that white churchmen believed not only that God created man in his own image but that God himself ordained the subjugation of blacks to whites. Hence slavery was of divine origin and was ordained to bring the subhuman blacks into association with a superior culture with the ultimate intent of saving their souls. The belief in white supremacy, however, was not restricted to the South, though it became more virulent there. Thus the post–Civil War restrictions placed upon Southern Negroes to keep a large segment of the population in a controlled environment for the benefit of a superior group had Northern endorsement. Northern hostility toward black people collectively is evidence of a continued moral support for Southern attitudes. Professor Smith has examined the role that Southern churches have played in the establishment of racism in the Bible Belt.[5] Credit for such an attitude, however, goes not to emotional Christianity alone but to most orthodox groups as well.

Richard Hofstadter in his *Anti-Intellectualism in American Life* states that many leaders of the right-wing groups in America have been preachers. He mentions Gerald Winrod of Kansas and J. Frank Norris of Texas, both antievolutionists; Carl McIntire, an opponent of modernism; and Gerald L. K. Smith. These, among others such as Billy James Hargis, have given inspiration to many Southern ministers who would preserve a *status quo*. "Studies of political intolerance and ethnic prejudice," writes Hofstadter, "have shown that zealous church-going and religious faith are among the important correlatives of political and ethnic animosity."[6]

The South's peculiar type of religion, however, should not be blamed for all its troubles. Nor should one generalize about Southern people, especially when the same traits may be observed elsewhere, but there are at least two distinct types. On the one hand, the older religiousness has produced a strong segment of pious folk whose spiritual growth has not kept pace with technological advancement and social change. But on the other hand, the "faith of our fathers" has populated the Southern sector with a great mass of citizens whose behavior reveals the more primitive and even animalistic traits that were apparent a century and a half ago when the frontier irreligiousness was being subdued. Some of these folk are paradoxical in nature—smug but insecure, pious but hypocritical, arrogant but frightened, law-abiding but tyrannical, hospitable but undemocratic.[7] They strive to win God's favor and recover their own self-confidence through either a crude ritual and incantation or a sterile formalism.

Persons of this paradoxical nature are very powerful because they are numerous and do not belong to a single social or economic group. Some may live in the more affluent residential areas or established neighborhoods, while others may exist in the slums or in dilapidated farmhouses. The latter have been referred to in the rural South by such names as "rednecks," "crackers," and "sharecroppers." In the urban South such a person is referred to as the common man or the Middle American, a member of either the blue- or the white-collar folk who, combined, comprise at least 60 percent of the population. These segments, urban and rural, in recent years have become identified with several groups. During the 1968 Presidential campaign some were identified by their George Wallace stickers on pickup trucks that sported gun racks. Others for years have been committed to the John Birch Society. Still others have affiliation with the Ku Klux Klan. Often their membership—other than to the church—is limited to the Rotary Club or the Lions Club or the local labor union. But politically they are increasingly identified as members of the hard-core radical right, with a twentieth-century adaptation of the older emotional religion that makes them comfortable and insulates them from outside ethical and moral pressure that would bring about change. Within this large cross section there may be differences between the persons involved, yet they have at least two similarities: they are frightened and they appear desperate in their efforts to preserve the *status quo*.

The more affluent, although fundamentalists in their religion, might be called one-hundred-percenters. Their hostility to change was seen during the New Deal when they resisted social reform. Now they are crying out against the welfare state, against "godless Communism," against the United Nations, against the income tax, and, finally, against desegregation of public facilities—especially in public education. The lower middle class are more concerned about the effects of civil rights legislation upon their economic status. Like their Civil War ancestors, they fear the effects of competition in the labor market. But both of these groups can trace their religious associations back to an earlier emotionalism in which they find a psychological basis for their attitudes and beliefs.

The religion that gave rise to the Bible Belt mystique had its origin in controversy. During the late eighteenth century and the first half of the nineteenth century, ministers throughout the section wrangled among themselves over a multitude of minutiae and over such larger principles as Baptism, free moral agency, depravity, and justification by faith alone through the atonement of Jesus Christ. Southerners came to view these concepts not only as doctrines but as inevitable categories of the human mind. As T. E. Hulme says in his *Speculations: Essays on Humanism and the Philosophy of Art:*

> Men do not look on them merely as correct opinion, for they have become so much a part of the mind, and lie so far back, that they are never really conscious of them at all. They do not see them, but other things *through* them. It is these abstract ideas at the centre, the things which they take for granted, that characterize a period.[8]

It was the defense of and protest against abstract things at the center, or doctrines taken as facts, which gave the religion of the early South its peculiar controversial nature. This led ultimately to shallow roots that usually did not supply the people with the kind of introspection or objectivity necessary to deal with the more complex problems then arising—for example, slavery, the higher criticism, Darwinism, and economic change.

Specifically, a faith that appealed primarily to the emotions lacked the depth to deal with the institution of slavery and Darwinian science. Instead, writes Reinhold Niebuhr, this emotionalism "sought to do justice to the impulse toward moral perfection by a scrupulous legalism, expressed in extravagant rules of Sabbath observance and a prurient attitude toward sex problems." It directed its attention also toward such things as intemperance, the use of tobacco, dancing, card-playing, theater-going, horse racing, cockfighting, and the reading of romantic novels. Southern evangelical Christianity took this direction in the first half of the nineteenth century, for it would not run aground on economic and political issues such as slavery. The power structure in the South set up limited and temporary objectives for its faith, and the churches have been slow in changing these goals. Niebuhr argues that such evangelical antidotes against secularism could not prove permanently effective because the religion was essentially emotional.[9] Hence the old-time religion carried forward into the twentieth century has been forced to adapt to the materialistic thinking which practical expediency and opportunism deemed necessary for progress in a highly competitive society, motivated by the compulsion for local control and a maximum in enjoyment of the gross national product. It has provided a sense of spiritual security, though some critics do accuse many of its converts of hypocrisy and selfishness.

How did this old-time religion acquire its peculiar

emotional characteristics? Why did it flourish in the agrarian and frontier region? Why did it endure? Is it today only a myth or a reality? Through an examination of history an effort will be made either to answer these questions or to help the reader arrive at his own conclusions from the assembled facts.

2

The Beginnings
of Southern Religiousness

IN 1882 WALTER HINES PAGE became editor and owner of the Raleigh *Chronicle*. He acknowledged the nobility of the South's past and paid tribute to its distinguished leadership before the Civil War, but he embraced the creed of a New South. His progressive views on the South's recovery of its greatness by industrialization and public education for the common man brought him into conflict with a type of conservatism that exists even today. He wrote editorials against the "ghosts" that were stifling progress in every Southern state, i.e., "the Ghost of the Confederate dead, the Ghost of religious orthodoxy, and the Ghost of Negro domination." These specters helped create a political and religious solidarity that has endured. The Confederate flag, emotional Christianity, and Jim Crowism, with all their connotations, are their symbols. Indeed, Southern behavior and thought have felt their influence because the phantoms were congenial.

The ghost of religious orthodoxy is the oldest of the three. It was conceived in an atmosphere of the spectacular, and a great segment of the lower middle and lower classes has continued to be identified with emotionalism, or revivalism. It has given Southern evangelical Christianity the special quality that is characterized in these pages.

The general theory and the various practices of revivalism, however, are not native to the Southern United States. They have been identified with the religion of Western civilization for hundreds of years. In a general sense, revivalism may even be traced to such Old Testament figures as Moses, Samuel, Hezekiah, and Ezra. The Feast of Tabernacles with its booths of green branches resembled the antebellum brush arbor. Certainly the purposes of leaders like Jesus, John the Baptist, and Paul bear a striking similarity to the objectives and endeavors of religionists during the period of the Old South and even into modern times. The history of Protestantism itself falls into three distinct revivals— the Reformation, Pietism, and Evangelicalism. By the middle of the seventeenth century, Puritanism was clearly reanimating the spiritually dead in England, and by the middle of the next century the evangelical revival under the leadership of Whitefield and the Wesleys was under way.

Revivalism became associated with the religious climate of America during the "Great Awakening" in New England (1734), and the revival of 1740 at Northampton, Massachusetts, under the direction of Jonathan Edwards, was influenced by certain techniques of George Whitefield. In his famous sermon, "Sinners in the Hands of an Angry God," Edwards merely substituted new images for some which he had heard Whitefield use very effectively, appealing to the emotions in an assault upon sin and those guilty of sin. Instead of calling the people "half beasts and half devils," Edwards followed a style which was equally devastating to self-confidence: "The God that holds you over the pit of Hell, much as we hold a spider, or some loathsome insect over the fire, abhors you, and is dreadfully provoked. His wrath towards you burns like fire." George Stanley Godwin in *The Great Revivalists* [1] points out that although Edwards adopted the method of scarification in order to flush out into the open any guilt-conscious or neurotic souls, he struck indirectly at Arminians and deists—two lawless, heretical, and blasphemous groups, as judged by orthodox Calvinistic standards. His objectives, techniques, and even the accompanying phenomena of his meetings anticipate those prevailing in the early period of the Old South and continuing in diminishing degree into the twentieth century. When the concept of an avenging God was replaced by that of a forgiving Jesus, when a boiling hell was replaced by one not geographically located, the tone of the sermons changed; still the most effective revivalists during the antebellum period, like Edwards, "stoked the furnaces of Hell." Not until after the Civil War was there any effort by the rural Baptist and Methodist pulpits to "bank the fires," which are still smoldering today in both country and city in some Protestant churches in lower-class neighborhoods.

Revivalism has been a contributing factor in shaping Southern religion. Its influence has perhaps been greater here than in other sections of America. By the time of the Civil War, much of the spectacle and extravaganza of the "Great Revival" (ca. 1799) was gone; however, the functions and some of the techniques have persisted. Philip Schaff observes in his book *America* (1855) that the flourishing period of revivalism is past and that even among Methodists the "swollen stream of religious excitement seems to be again seeking its natural, fixed channels, especially in the more cultivated city congregations," which, he adds, have never really approved of such unwholesome excesses.[2] His negative judgment reflects something of Episcopalian and later Presbyterian reaction to undue show of emotion in church services.

Between 1840 and 1844 a second general revival of religion swept throughout America, affecting the South and old Southwest (the Deep South) perhaps more than elsewhere. It found expression in numerous prayer meetings and sacramental services, eventually culminating in a series of camp meetings. James Porter in his *A Compendium of Methodism* attributed this condition primarily to the "out-pouring of the Spirit of God upon the public heart." Another cause to which this general revival was attributed was the widespread belief that the second coming of Jesus was close at hand. In fact, some predicted the date as 1843; William Miller, the millennial prophet, argued for 1847.[3] To be sure, the popularity of religion increased tremendously on the eve of the anticipated event and declined a little when the prophecy was not fulfilled. Still another cause of this widespread emotionalism, as Methodists and Baptists argued, was a decadent condition, attributed particularly to Episcopalian and Presbyterian churches, which had been charged with certain "freezing operations." Congregations had grown cold on sermons of a theological nature because they appealed less to the heart than to the mind. Emotionalism, rather than rationalism, was essential in the religion of frontier and agrarian folk.

The people who settled the Southern frontiers in the late eighteenth century had few aesthetic, cultural, or intellectual interests. They were close to nature in the rough, combating the numerous forces and obstacles in their environment. The "survival of the fittest" was an applicable law that governed the daily lives of the settlers. Engaged in a life-and-death struggle with nature to provide the minimum in food, clothing, and shelter for large families (increasing almost yearly), man's passions became elemental. To be sure, as historians Henry Kallock Rowe and William Warren Sweet suggest, they reacted emotionally rather than intellectually to their religion.[4] The more informal services suited their temperament and needs, their preference for excitement and for the bizarre. Among such folk, revivalism was destined to secure a firm footing in the South and the old Southwest and to be particularly popular for more than sixty years. However, there have been no fewer than five distinct periods since 1798, each lasting perhaps not more than a decade, when the people have made a concerted effort to motivate a general, regional excitement.

The evolvement of the new religiousness was by no means to take place with harmony among the various sects. For instance, Episcopalians and Presbyterians accused Methodists, in particular, of conjuring up false spirits or devils in their camp meetings under the guise of the Holy Spirit. Some of the complaints were that those sects, relying upon certain artificial techniques to effect conversion on a mass scale, were guilty of provoking spurious religious excitements. The assumption was that the churches would have a mass of unregenerates on their rolls when so many would return to the ranks of the wicked after the effects of the mushroom profession of faith had worn off.

As a safeguard against such criticism, specific standards were set for converts. Certain changes in the inner self were deemed essential. Writing for the *Western Baptist Review* in 1849, John M. Peck states the problem in clerical terms. First, he says, man's heart had to be renewed or rededicated; secondly, the Holy Spirit had to be present; and thirdly, means employed to produce a revival of religion had to be in accordance with the Scriptures.[5] Therefore, man had to experience a genuine rejuvenation before the results would be acceptable.

Near the end of the eighteenth century the stage was being set. The frontier had never really felt the influence of a religion, and when the pious observed the demoralizing effects of the American Revolution, they became aware of the need for spiritual stimulation. Bibles were so scarce that in 1816 the American Bible

Society felt compelled to distribute free copies among farmers. There were so few preachers that the people were like sheep without a shepherd.

The general reasons for this condition are numerous, but a basic and philosophical one is to be found in the Enlightenment. On the Continent, especially in France, considerable opposition to the Bible had developed. Ministers seemed to do a great deal of rationalizing when they showed that emperors, kings, and popes had justified their "bloody inquisitions" upon Scriptural grounds. The people generally had become soured upon "God's Word," primarily because their leaders had taken undue liberties with the divine writings. Preachers, however, both in America and abroad, in the face of widespread criticism, tried to appeal to common sense to show that the Bible was not at fault, that the sources of evil lay in the misuse of inspired writings. Nevertheless, in spite of all that the pulpit could do, indifference, encouraged by a general optimism where land was free and the individual was self-sufficient, continued to spread.

Religious rationalism, which led to the formulation of deism, had its beginning in the sixteenth century among the Socinians, but not until the next century in England was the religion of reason crystallized. The deists came to be regarded as unorthodox and radical. The personalities associated with the new liberalism were Lord Herbert of Cherbury, John Toland, and Anthony Collins. Although they were not properly deists, the names of Lord Shaftesbury, Mandeville, and Lord Bolingbroke also appear. Ministerial tracts of the Old South mention more often, however, the names of Voltaire, Rousseau, and Paine. J. H. Spencer, a prominent historian for the Kentucky Baptists, writes that Voltaire, disgusted with the corruptions and oppressions of the religion of his own country, set out to destroy "the religion of Christ" in the whole world.[6] With a belief in the innate goodness of man instead of allegiance to the traditional view of natural depravity (from the imputation of Adam's sin upon the human race), Rousseau was also associated with these so-called contaminators of Christendom. According to the Southern pulpit, though, Tom Paine was the "biggest scoundrel" of them all, for in the midst of this era of so-called "spiritual darkness" came his book *The Age of Reason.* He wrote: "You have thrown off the allegiance to the British king; now throw off the yoke of superstition, and be freemen indeed." Not prepared to accept such liberalism, Americans—clerical and secular—condemned him vehemently, reacting as did James Gallaher in *The Western Sketch-Book:*

> Paine scoffed at all that was sacred in religion—profanely mocked and blasphemed the ordinances of God. O, it was a tremendous eruption of the bottomless pit! The shock had well nigh thrown down the hope of the church. The smoke that ascended filled all the air with blackness, and eclipsed the sun; while ashes, cinders and lava came down, threatening to bury every vestige of good that yet remained in society.[7]

While Methodists were belligerent toward Paine, they were confident of ultimate victory over all such opposition, as is revealed in the following verse from a popular song reported by Charles A. Johnson in *The Frontier Camp Meeting, Religion's Harvest Time:*

> The *world,* the Devil and Tom Paine
> Have try'd their force, but all in vain,
> They can't prevail, the reason is,
> The Lord defends the Methodist.[8]

Robert Davidson in his book on Presbyterianism laments conditions in Kentucky:

> The prospect was sufficiently gloomy to appall both the Christian and the patriot. . . . Worldly-mindedness, infi-

delity, and dissipation threatened to deluge the land, and sweep away all vestiges of piety and morality. The rising generation were growing up in almost universal ignorance of religious obligation.[9]

As a compromise between science and orthodox theology, deism contained certain elements that appealed to intellectuals who attempted to maintain church affiliation. For instance, deists believed in immortality and in one God, but in a Creator who had produced through a set of immutable laws a nature that he was powerless to change without admitting his own imperfection. Deists showed further that men share in cosmic harmony. In agreement with the followers of Rousseau, they added that man is innately good, that evil stems from social institutions and civilization. Significant, too, was their insistence upon the freedom of the individual will, in this agreeing with Arminianism but opposing Calvinism. However, orthodox preachers, Arminians and Calvinists, swarmed all over the deists when they denied the implications of the Trinity, divine providence, the divinity of Christ, and the divine inspiration of the Scriptures. (Unitarianism was the next step in the development of this type of liberalism.) Calvinists in particular became aroused when their doctrines of predestination, election, and total depravity were sharply challenged by this new cult of liberal thinkers.

However, Tom Paine's *The Age of Reason* was not the only tract that was associated with fostering impiety. To name a few: In 1784, Ethan Allen published his attack on revealed religion, *Reason the Only Oracle of Man;* Elihu Palmer set forth his infidelism in *Principles of Nature* (1802); and Thomas Jefferson translated Constantin Volney's *Ruins, or a Survey of the Revolution of Empires,* which related Christianity to Eastern religions.

Quite naturally the popularity of things religious declined during the systematic onslaught of deism through books, pamphlets, and newspapers. *The Theophilanthropist* and *The Temple of Reason* were newspapers sponsored by societies in New York and Philadelphia. Especially along the frontier religion seemed on the decline. In 1800 probably not more than 5 percent of Southerners were affiliated with a church. From most pulpits came the cry that the truth of the Bible was everywhere being questioned; and for this reason there was vigorous preaching against those who seemed to support unorthodox beliefs. Protests against infidelity, blasphemy, immorality, indifference, and ignorance—all synonymous with deism in the eyes of most preachers—followed in the wake of the new liberalism.

Men, made insensible to human and cultural values by their constant struggle with nature—the stubborn land, wildlife, and hostile Indians—became similarly resistant to spiritual values when all about them were heretical ideas and bitter charges against the Scriptures. Some were escapees from an Eastern religious culture, and as Merton E. Coulter explains in his *College Life in the Old South*, "Those who fled the 'hellfire and brimstone' eruptions of the Jonathan Edwardses of the older settlements were not anxious that the religion they had left behind should soon catch up with them." [10] The people were very often revelers in the so-called unchristian activities of cockfighting, drinking, dueling, gambling, and horse racing. Peter Cartwright, the celebrated Methodist circuit rider, recalled that when his father moved to the frontier community of "Rogues Harbor" in 1793 the majority of the citizens were murderers, horse thieves, highway robbers, counterfeiters, fugitive bond servants, and runaway debtors. Such a motley crew could neither know nor recognize restraints, legal or religious. Cartwright added that to enforce the law a minority organized "The Regulators," who fought several unsuccessful pitched battles with the "rogues" before order was restored.[11] Although Timothy Dwight—poet, theologian, and president of Yale—had observed similar rowdyism in his section, travelers from the East and from abroad discovered what was to them an unwholesome flavor in the South, especially along the frontiers. For example, Charles Crossfield Ware in his biography of Barton W. Stone reports Josiah Espy as saying:

> The state of society in Kentucky I did not admire. The great body of the well informed and wealthy were immersed in infidelity and dissipation, while the more illiterate were downright fanatics and zealots in religion. However, they are generally an hospitable people and polite to strangers. With a few exceptions they are more sprightly and fonder of conversation than Pennsylvanians and have a remarkable attachment to all public meetings and amusements, particularly to horse-racing, where they assemble in vast crowds.[12]

However, at this time the behavior which preachers believed immoral was very often a part of the gentleman's code. For example, drinking, dueling, gambling, and horse racing were fashionable, but not respected by most churches. There were, then, two standards, but the code of the pulpit by 1855 came to be clearly accepted by the masses. This change may be attributed partly to the impact of the repeated revivals upon Southern folk.

Certain conditions in the church and community helped motivate the "Great Revival." Davidson noted that a decided majority of the people in the "Cumberland Country" were reputed to be infidels, and he affirmed that since infidelity was the prolific parent of vice it was not surprising to find the whole country remarkable for sin and dissipation. He criticized the church for not throwing up barriers to check infidelity and vice, and he pointed out that it had become impotent from covetousness or wasting its energies in frivolous disputes.[13] The elder clergy were scarce, with the majority in their dotage, while many others were mediocre or untrained. Too many members had become indifferent to religious ceremonies. Only the older persons approached the communion, while the young showed no concern whatever. According to Spencer, the Presbyterian David Rice could scarcely believe his eyes when he found so many lifeless and reckless people pretending to belong to the church. He says:

I found scarcely one man, and but few women, who supported a credible profession of religion. Some were grossly ignorant of the first principles of religion. Some were given to quarreling and fighting, some to profane swearing, some to intemperance, and perhaps most of them totally negligent of the forms of religion in their own houses. I could not think a church formed of such materials as these could properly be called a church of Christ. With this I was considerably distressed, and made to cry, where am I! What situation am I in? [14]

T. C. Blake, a Cumberland Presbyterian preacher, also presents a gloomy picture of the frontier. There were ministers living in the settled portions of the South, some even learned men, who persisted in delivering cold, formal, and lifeless sermons. They talked too much, Blake writes, of the "elect of God" and said little about the "new birth"—"the religion of the heart." The gospel had a "savor of death unto death" instead of "a savor of life unto life." He frankly states that some of the ministers were not converted men. For instance, James McGready, who shared in setting off the "Great Revival," was one who had preached for several years before he became a confirmed Christian. The sudden transformation which later occurred in McGready's life and sermonizing illustrates the change that came over the whole section through the influence of revivalism. After his conversion, instead of pursuing

the rational and theological emphasis that had characterized pulpit techniques of the preceding century,
McGready spoke in "thunder tones" to the wayward,
saying, "Ye must be born again." Also significant was
his insistence that sinners should know the *time when*
and the *place where* they were converted.[15] This new
view of conversion became very popular among
agrarian and pioneering peoples.

The purpose of the sermon was what it had been in
the seventeenth and eighteenth centuries—to persuade
the hearer to view honestly the condition of his soul. To
achieve this goal the pulpit preached the gospel of
Jesus Christ with the hope of moving the people to realize the importance of faith and regeneration, and with
a further hope of bringing within the individual's soul
the triumph of good over evil, the spirit over the flesh,
and God over the devil. The point at stake was merely a
change in techniques necessitated by the wave of
antireligiousness and anti-intellectualism within the
sparsely settled regions. The transition was from
rationalism (formal theology) to empiricism, from a
religion of the mind to one of the heart. Revivalism was
the movement destined to foster this development and
drive infidelity and a nineteenth-century type of sin
from the Southern heart.

The Methodists became the nursemaid of the revival
movement, while the Presbyterians and the Baptists
were the parents. The Presbyterians, perhaps, can best
claim to have introduced the new approach to religion,
because the camp meeting as conceived in America actually began in one of their services. Too, they were the
first to discover the decadent elements in their own
churches and to begin searching for a cure. But so controversial became the techniques that those Presbyterians who held any regard for the new approaches to
salvation found themselves unwelcomed among the
solid core of their denomination. As a result they broke

away to organize a presbytery in southwestern Kentucky, where McGready was active. They formed what later became known as the Cumberland Presbyterian Church. Meanwhile, by attacking Barton Stone and Richard McNemar, the conservatives precipitated another schism (in 1803–1804), resulting in the departure of some who were popularly known as "New Lights." Methodists apparently attracted more of the later revivalists, for Wesley and Whitefield had already sanctioned the methods which came to be associated with the extravagant techniques.

More than a decade before the "Great Revival" of 1799 got under way there were sporadic upheavals along the frontier; for instance, Baptists in Kentucky enjoyed some degree of spiritual prosperity near the end of 1785. Ministers were holding meetings more frequently in the cabins of settlers, and congregations were increasing in size. More important, though, was the expression of greater tenderness of feeling and some weeping during preaching services. In John Craig's settlement on Clear Creek (in what became Woodford County) considerable emotionalism was apparent, its influence having been felt in other neighborhoods. For the two succeeding years, Baptist congregations all through Kentucky experienced new impulses that changed the despondency of religionists to optimism, because they believed they were gaining ground against the indifference of the frontier. John Waller, for example, inspired a great revival of religion in which many hundreds were baptized, the general effects spreading through his section of the country and continuing for several years.[16] This upheaval reached as far as Virginia, with similar activities reported in other states of the South and old Southwest.

In 1789 at Craig's Station, Garrard County, there occurred something of the type of hysteria that was to characterize the meetings of the next decade. The scene was an Arminian Baptist church at Gilbert's Creek, under the ministry of Joseph Bledsoe and his son William. The pulpit had warned the people time and again that they were all going to hell, and Bledsoe (though probably the victim of some prankster) produced great excitement by displaying publicly two hen eggs upon which were written the sentence, "The Day of God's Awful Judgment Is Near." As he read this evidence of the approaching doom, he seemed alarmed. With no tongue in cheek J. H. Spencer described the fear among the people and the great excitement that led to about four hundred being added to the church.[17]

The progress of revivalism was hindered a great deal by the scarcity of preachers, but with the increasing demand for religious teaching, prayer meetings were held by laymen in the homes of both rich and destitute. Although many of these inexperienced missionaries had never before spoken in public, some of their exhortations proved to be very effective. In such meetings there was much singing of a devotional character, old and young blending their voices with a zeal that has hardly been equaled in American church history. Thus "coals of the spirit" were kept alive until there were enough trained or lay ministers to fan the flame into what very shortly became a conflagration.

The forces that set off the "Great Revival" of 1799 had their beginning in the month of May 1797, which was the spring after James McGready came to this country. The people of the Gasper River congregation in Kentucky were inquiring seriously about the doctrines of regeneration, faith, and repentance, which McGready was regularly preaching. McGready states that all through the winter "the question was often proposed to me, Is Religion a sensible thing? If I were converted would I feel it, and know it?" [18] His account of the evolution of religious feeling along the frontier shows something of the increasing intensity. The first convert was a woman who found herself out of step with Christian ideals. After she was struck with deep conviction, she began going from house to house telling of her experience, creating throughout the countryside a note of uneasiness, upon which McGready and others capitalized. He recalls that his sermons now began to awaken sinners, but he admits that months passed before he became aware of any success. In the summer of 1798, at the administration of the sacrament of the Lord's Supper, the people were notably more conscious of their lost estate, and on the first Sunday of September at Muddy River many were even talking about the condition of their souls. However, there was a slight retarding of McGready's work by opposition from an antirevivalist group, led by James Balch; but the confusion that resulted soon passed, for by July 1799 something important seemed to be taking place. These were the events that set the stage for the "Great Revival" and the introduction of the celebrated camp meetings in America.

These events actually happened through the combined efforts of two brothers, John and William McGee—the one a Methodist local preacher and the other an ordained Presbyterian—who had been called by the congregation in Sumner (later Smith) County, Tennessee. Before coming to Tennessee from North Carolina, both men had received good training in a Presbyterian theological seminary. In this almost unbroken wilderness, six days a week they tilled the soil on adjoining farms, and on the seventh they served in their respective pulpits. However, their most sensational endeavors were in the adjoining state of Kentucky, at the Red River meetinghouse in Logan County, under the charge of James McGready. After the custom of the times they had requested appointments, and when the two brothers arrived they were met by McGready, John Rankin, and William Hoge. Though the meeting was scheduled to be a sacramental occasion, there were ominous signs on the horizon of bigger developments. T. Marshall Smith writes that on Saturday, William McGee delivered a sermon designed to prepare the people for participation in the eucharistic feast on the next day. Then on Sunday, Hoge delivered the sermon in the forenoon, addressing the assembly with a freedom and a power that he had never before experienced. The listeners were silent and attentive.

As soon as he closed his sermon, John McGee, scheduled to follow him in the pulpit, arose singing:

> "Come, Holy Spirit, heavenly Dove,
> With all Thy quickening powers;
> Kindle a flame of sacred love
> In these cold hearts of ours."

Scarcely had he finished before two elderly ladies, a Mrs. Pacely, sitting across the congregation to his left, and a Mrs. Clark, on the opposite side of the church, began a dialogue in rather subdued but distinct tones of voice. They offered praise to the "Most High" for "His grace and goodness in redemption." McGee sang on, and the ladies grew increasingly louder in their praises of God. Continuing to sing, he walked down out of the pulpit to shake hands with them, and en route grasped the hands of all within his reach. Then occurred some of the phenomena that characterized the camp meetings of the early nineteenth century: "Instantly they fell as he progressed through the crowd—some as dead men and women—some most piteously crying for mercy, and a few, here and there, lifting their voices high in the praise of the Redeemer." Even William McGee, who fell to the floor shouting praises, was so completely "overpowered with the divine afflatus" that he could not regain his feet. So surprised were the other ministers that they hurried out of the meetinghouse for consultation; they had never before seen such confusion.

Petrified, they stood there, whispering to one another, until Hoge ventured back to peek through the door, where he beheld nearly everyone on the floor, either praying or shouting praises to the Lord. Turning to his companions, he said: "We can do nothing. If this be of Satan, it will soon come to an end. But if of God, our efforts and fears are vain! I think it is of God, and will join in giving glory to His name." [19]

Returning to the spectacle, they continued to be startled by the strange behavior, because some who had fallen to the floor moaning and crying for mercy rose, frequently two or more at exactly the same moment. They always came up "shouting praises for the evidences they felt in their souls of sins forgiven—for 'redeeming grace, and dying love!' " The original plans for administering the sacrament were now abandoned, because the feeling was too strong for the restoration of order. At the evening service, between thirty and forty professed conversion.

On the following weekend the McGee brothers held services at the Beech meetinghouse, located seventeen miles northeast of Nashville. The strange phenomena of the preceding week naturally brought hundreds to the service—some to seek divine favor, others "to witness, analyze, and expose what they were pleased to stigmatize with the stereotyped brands of infidelity in every land, . . . and in all ages, *'fanaticism, wildfire*, and *hypocrisy.'* " At the eleven o'clock service on Sunday, a similar crisis was reached in this religious drama. Before John McGee had finished his sermon, hundreds of people began falling, rejoicing, or pleading for mercy.

The climax, however, actually came the next week at Muddy River, three miles east of Russellville; and it was on this occasion that the big meeting in the out-of-doors came into being. Likewise it was at these services that McGready discovered a certain uniqueness about the moment of a penitent's conversion, for he now realized that he had been preaching for years without having undergone the experience. He too was seen "among those crying for mercy," and he explained that never before had he felt the "scriptural assurance that he was born of God." [20]

Although slow at first in responding to what revivalists called "the Spirit," the Southern frontier became an open conflagration with the first few conversions. The whole area became extremely excited. The kindling point in a great religious awakening had been reached. The "Great Revival" was on!

After these first phenomenal demonstrations, which influenced immeasurably Southern behavior and thought for many years, there were sporadic outbursts, which illustrate how revivalism operates. For example, change sometimes occurred so slowly that the participants were unaware of the approaching crisis. The following episode, years later, shows how the revival affected a typical antebellum community where no special effort was made to produce excitement. In January 1826, N. Hoyt, the minister for a small and destitute Presbyterian congregation in South Carolina, found moral dearth and desolation everywhere. However, attracting a large audience on the Sabbath was no problem at all, with no other organized denominations in the vicinity to draw the people elsewhere. When he took over the pastorate he found no Sabbath school, no praying men anywhere around, and no family prayer to speak of. Sunday was desecrated by visiting, recreation, profane swearing, intemperance, and ignorance of religious matters. Hoyt labored for about four months, organizing a Bible class, distributing tracts, and conducting prayer services in the homes. Although he met kindness and hospitality, he had nothing positive to show for his efforts. Not a single conversion did he have during these months of preaching, and success in the ministry within an evangelical religion has always been partially measured by the number of souls saved and new names added to the church roster. Autumn faded into winter, and winter gave way to spring, but, lamented Hoyt, still no sinners had turned to God. The people heard the sweet caroling of the mockingbird and the soothing voice of the turtledove; they noted that nature was in a festive mood. The people responded to the general cheerfulness of the out-of-doors, but

> there was one who was far from being happy; one, whom no music of nature, nor kindness of friends could cheer; one, from whose eyes sleep departed at night, and upon whose mind there daily rested a mountain pressure, which no one but the Almighty could remove. It was the preacher. . . . He was made to see as clearly as in the blaze of the noonday sun, that the people with whom he was laboring were going to hell.[21]

Then almost instantly a deep solemnity came over the congregation. "The Holy Ghost breathed upon the valley, and the dry bones began to move, to tremble, and to shake." After one hundred years of existence the little community had its first conversion; the mother of a very large family, with no apparent forewarning, arose and walked down to the pulpit to give Hoyt her hand. It would seem that the congregation had collectively been experiencing the same emotion, for immediately every man, woman, and child arose and crowded after her. All made their way to the altar, weeping and sobbing. Hoyt had indulged in no special pleading, using only the calm and rational approach that characterized his usual Presbyterian sermons. Although there was less demonstration of ecstasy and animal feeling than that manifested in most of the services where such results occurred, the revival spirit was kept alive.

The revival began first in individuals who were greatly troubled in their souls. They reacted in strange ways; some even cried out, others talked with their neighbors, and still others experienced an inward throbbing of the heart, followed by weeping and trembling, then perhaps a falling down and even swooning. In his *Western Sketch-Book,* Gallaher recalls that, while the minister Dobbins was preaching one morning, two young men of respectable families, well-known in the congregation, began to tremble in their seats; stubborn sinners were struck down like Saul (Paul) on his way to Damascus.[22] The instantaneous conversion was a frequent occurrence during these periods of greatest religious activity.

Beginning in 1800 there was an emigration to the West and South of missionaries from the East and the Atlantic seaboard. At one time or another came Baptists, Methodists, Disciples, Presbyterians, and even a few Episcopalians. Some of them had received a formal education; others had little learning or worldly goods, and as the uncertainties of the frontier demanded, they may have come with a rifle in one hand, but a Bible in the other. They all crossed over the mountains and descended upon the frontier with a common purpose—to chase the devil out of the wilderness. To be sure, the laborers were few, but their courage and enthusiasm offset many personal deficiencies and material shortages. Naturally, in the language of the parable, they scattered some of their seeds among the thorns and on stony ground, but those seeds which fell on fertile soil—on receptive hearts—and were not eaten by the fowls of the air grew to produce a great harvest, as the later religiousness of Southern people seems to testify.

3

The Eruption of Salvation

ALTHOUGH no more than one hundred and fifty years have passed since the Southern camp meeting became a reality, historians continue to reflect upon the scene with the strange revival phenomena.

The Southern pulpit believed that the camp meeting sprang into existence almost instantaneously out of conventional religious services, the number of conversions often exceeding ministerial expectations. In effectiveness and in spectacle it was phenomenal, unprecedented in church history. It was illustrative of the times, of the people, and of their peculiar responsiveness to an emotional type of religion. No other section of America could match the South with such an eruption. Essayists, poets, novelists, biographers, and clerics were prolific in discussing the origin, setting, and appearance of camp meetings and in their accounts of freakish conversions and religious "exercises," as they were popularly called.

Camp meetings, contemporaries contended, originated in the West—in Kentucky and Tennessee—though the exact date has been disputed by historians. They did not come about as the result of a carefully laid plan, nor did they originate among the Methodists, who after 1805 have been associated with this new type of worship. By 1825 the camp meeting had become almost entirely a Methodist institution, but it had its origin among the Presbyterians, growing out of regularly scheduled sacramental ceremonies. When there was an exhibition of the Holy Ghost, the meeting was "protracted" and the word was passed around through the area until sometimes great multitudes assembled for the spiritual feast. When the crowds became so great that the meetinghouse could no longer hold them, they went into the woods or an open field, sometimes erecting temporary quarters and living on provisions brought from homes or provided by the local church people. This type of worship became so effective that Methodists carried it into other sections of America. Baptists likewise made use of this popular custom. It survives today in the city under the big tent, in small communities perhaps at the fairgrounds or on some vacant acreage generally set aside for traveling shows and circuses. The brush arbor meetings of the minor sects, such as the Nazarenes and the Pentecostals, are also survivals.

The first camp meeting in America was probably the one at Muddy River in 1799. John and William McGee, referred to earlier, had attracted attention because of the strange responses. On this particular occasion the meetinghouse was full hours before the appointed time for the service to begin, and with only one third of the crowd provided for. People continued to come by the hundreds. A temporary pulpit was erected under the trees and a few seats were provided by cutting down some of the timber in the forest. The preaching had scarcely begun when many people began crying for mercy, others shouting for joy. Even church members were scattered all over the ground along with the so-called sinners. Those living near Muddy River suddenly realized that night was approaching and there was no way to disperse a mob of "seekers of salvation every moment increasing." Eight or ten of the leaders came together to consider the matter of food and shelter for the multitude. They then sent three or four wagons to the surrounding yards and barns for straw to spread on the ground. They put some people to sewing wagon sheets together, others to cutting forks and poles for the tents. They dispatched still others to town and to the nearest houses to gather bacon, flour, and meal, and the cooking utensils essential to prepare food for the great horde, which had reached several thousand in number. Within a few hours the whole area had undergone a change: straw was scattered over half an acre, a large tent covered the pulpit, ten or twelve smaller tents were arranged in order around the ground where the straw was spread, and people were standing and sitting. T. Marshall Smith writes: "Fires were built, cooking begun, and by dark, candles lighted and fixed on a hundred trees around and interspersing the ground surrounded by the tents, showing forth the *first* . . . camp meetings the world has ever seen." [1]

The camp meeting soon became a Southern institution. A composite picture of an antebellum site included a grove of trees and a running stream for the water supply. Localities often set aside acreage as a permanent campground. Very likely the more prominent settlers became "tent-holders"; committees were appointed to lay plans for what came to be popularly known as "religious cities" to assure that tents or cottages were uniform and properly situated. D. Sullins in *Recollections of an Old Man* reminisces about a typical campground at Cedar Springs, Tennessee, where Methodists held their "religious rallies." Here was a small log church and a shed 125 feet long and 75 feet wide, with wings on hinges, so that when they were up some two thousand could be seated. Surrounding the buildings were rude shacks of logs with no fireplaces, beds of scaffolds along the walls, and dirt floors covered with straw. Sullins preferred straw to sawdust, since he associated it with the smell of fields and the ring of the reaper's blades; it connoted, too, certain cherished memories and associations of his childhood.[2] Straw reminded others of the stable scene in Bethlehem. Sometimes, instead of the surrounding log shacks, small tents were used, and a place was set aside for cooking where there were furnaces or bonfires. Between the trees were stretched many small lamps, and immediately around the meeting place were containers of pine knots soaked in pitch which when lighted burned brightly and gave off a smoke that helped drive away mosquitoes. Though the lighting was primitive and gave the environs a weird overcast, it compared favorably with the Aladdin lamps and gas lamps of a later period, when pavilions, sheds, and auditoriums supplanted many of the old amphitheaters, tabernacles, brush arbors, and simple clearings in the forests. In front of the platform—on which sometimes twenty or thirty preachers sat—was a straw-covered enclosure for the "mourners' benches," as followers of Alexander Campbell called them in contempt.[3] In a sense they were scenes of much mourning, moaning, and groaning; but ultimately they were scenes of great happiness.

Regardless of denomination, there were rather uniform regulations. One side of the ground was set aside for women and the other for men. Even during services the sexes were separated, in the hope of creating a more dignified atmosphere. At night women were not permitted to leave their quarters after a certain hour. Persons waking before morning were allowed to pray or sing if they exercised restraint. A horn or bell was sounded about dawn as a signal for the people to arise and to prepare breakfast. The next signal was for services to begin; and since there was a crowded schedule, often four sermons daily, worshipers were required to assemble quickly and to observe all the rules of the camp meeting manual.

At these assemblies one would find a cross section of Southern society. The ambitious and wealthy attended, if not to gain a stronger grasp on the world to come, at least to extend their influence in the present, fearing that their absence might diminish it. Politicians were present to electioneer among the multitudes. Many curiosity seekers came just for the spectacle. Besides these, according to Timothy Flint,

> the young and the beautiful [were] there, with mixed motives, which it were best not severely to scrutinize. Children [were] there, their young eyes glistening with the intense interest of eager curiosity. The middle aged fathers and mothers of families [were] there, with the sober views of people, whose plans in life [were] fixed, and waiting calmly to hear. Men and women of hoary hairs [were] there, with such thoughts, it may be hoped, as their years invite.[4]

A good number of preachers, frequently of different denominations, might be on hand, some veterans of many meetings, and some neophytes, with only enthusiasm and no experience or training. Certainly there were those who frequented the outskirts of the grounds: bootleggers, gamblers, cockfighters, horse racers, prostitutes, jailbirds, pickpockets, highwaymen, and rowdies—the dregs of society.

People came from distances as far as fifty or one hundred miles, in coaches, chaises, wagons, carts, on foot, and on horseback. Those who camped on the grounds brought provisions and bedding, prepared to stay the full period—from four days to a week. These services could last for a longer period and thus the term "protracted meeting" was coined. It was an occasion that everyone, old and young alike, looked forward to. Robert Davidson reminisces thus:

> The laborer quitted his task; age snatched his crutch; youth forgot his pastime; the plough was left in the fur-

row; the deer enjoyed a respite upon the mountains; business of all kinds was suspended; dwelling houses were deserted; whole neighborhoods were emptied; bold hunters and sober matrons, young men, maidens and little children, flocked to the common centre of attraction.[5]

Aside from an occasional Saturday or Sunday service, house-raisings, logrollings, quilting parties, and spelling bees, there was little other amusement to break the monotony of clearing land, plowing, planting, and harvesting crops. Thus the camp meeting served a social as well as a spiritual function. It was a gala occasion and a "king cure-all."

At almost any sort of meeting one would find scores of horses tied to fences and trees, with many wagons and carriages standing around. According to Timothy Flint, "The woods and paths seemed alive with people, and the number reported as attending is almost incredible." The larger meetings, like those at Cane Ridge, attracted from ten to twenty thousand. Davidson prepared a set of statistics to show the gigantic nature of these activities. Counting the number of vehicles on the ground, he found 143 carriages and wagons, 500 covered sleighs, or sledges, and 500 without covers—a total of 1,143 conveyances. He also counted 500 candles, besides lamps, used to illuminate the camp at night.[6] James Gallaher, who was also statistically-minded, estimated that there were 20,000 people at this famous meeting. He said he saw at least 140 wagons, besides other wheel carriages, which came loaded with passengers.[7] With so many people in one gathering, without modern amplifying systems, often there had to be several speakers' stands. Perhaps as many as four services were conducted simultaneously, arranged so that no audience would be distracted by activities in another.

An old Southern camp meeting beggars description.

The many accounts by western travelers all affirm that they had never beheld anything like it. Neighboring preachers were known to leave their circuits and give assistance in these "pitched battles" with the devil. Before denominational lines became so tightly drawn, Methodists, Presbyterians, and Baptists often pooled their manpower, the latter group becoming less willing, however, because of their prejudice against sprinkling as a method of baptism and their common practice of closed communion. Finally, the "Old Side" Presbyterians frequently refused to cooperate, but the Cumberland Presbyterians and "New Lights" ("Stonites," as they were referred to by some) remained friendly to the ideas behind the new emotionalism. Hence the Methodists often found themselves working independently in their use of a technique that they did not originate but that has come to be associated with them. William Warren Sweet says the camp meeting really never became an official Methodist institution; yet, no one in later years questioned its identity with Methodism.[8]

As stated above, the blowing of a horn or ringing of a bell started activities. After breakfast, which no doubt included corn pone and jerked meat without salt, the meeting always began with prayers and the singing of sonorous tunes. The woods reverberated with the pealing rhythm of the hymns. Sermon followed sermon, and prayer followed prayer. On the rostrum a "son of thunder" walked up and down stalking the devil, crying to sinners (some of whom were already lying in the straw at the mourners' bench), "Now is the accepted time!" "Call upon him while he is near!" His assistants moved through the crowd, watching for any display of emotion and from time to time shouting, "Tell it to 'em, brother!" The crowd became more and more excited, clapping their hands and shouting, "Amen!" "Bless the Lord!" "Glory to God!" "Glory! Hallelujah!"

At a moment when the emotion of the crowd seemed

about to burst, the preacher, who was ranting on the platform, might do something sensational. John McGee once asked the congregation to shout if they wanted to go to heaven. Frequently when the crowd was seething with excitement and fear, the preacher on the rostrum might lead a march around the grounds singing a magnificent song or, as in the case of a particular Methodist meeting, rude adaptations such as the following:

> The Devil hates the Methodists:
>   O halle—halleluia;
> Because they do keep so much fuss,
>   O glory halleluia.

And:

> Shout! shout! we are gaining ground
>   O halle—halleluia.
> The Devil's kingdom shall come down:
>   O glory halleluia! [9]

Or he might use the then popular songs to show, for example, the utility of prayer:

> The richest man I ever saw was one that
>   begged the most,
> His soul was filled with glory and with the
>   Holy Ghost,
> And a-begging I will go—will go—will go! [10]

T. W. Caskey recalls an instance, reported in *Seventy Years in Dixie*. The preacher asked the three thousand who had assembled whether they wanted "to go to heaven," and if so to respond by clapping their hands as one man when he gave the signal. As one might suspect, the response to such a request as this was always in the affirmative. The preacher learned to his sorrow that the "gate to heaven" was too narrow for such an open invitation. Caskey writes:

It sounded like a thunderbolt and a yell of "glory" almost loud enough to wake the dead. The effect was almost electrical. Scores of sinners shrieked for mercy in
all parts of the vast audience, hundreds of happy Christians raised wild shouts of joy and the rest of the surging
crowd united their voices in a familiar song. The negro
slaves were coming from all parts of the country to the
meeting, and were scattered all over the woods for a mile
around the camp-ground, when the storm of fuss and excitement burst under the arbor. The noise frightened
them and they began to shriek for mercy and pray aloud
all over the woods, in the darkness, as though the devil
himself were at their heels. There were hundreds of
dogs in the camp, as usual, and, excited by the unusual
noise and confusion, they rushed into the woods and the
darkness in every direction, yelping as if a whole menag-
erie of wild beasts had been suddenly let loose among
them. In a few moments they raised a free fight and a
general row among themselves, and every dog on the
grounds rushed into the fray. When the canine forces
were all mustered, there was probably a square acre of
yelping, snapping, fighting dogs within a few rods of the
arbor. There were several hundred horses, mules, oxen,
and wagons on the grounds, and the unusual confusion,
fuss and excitement stampeded these animals. The scene
beggars description. Three thousand people in an
uproar, hundreds of dogs yelping and fighting, negroes
screaming and praying in every direction, and frightened
mules, horses and oxen dashing madly through the
woods in the darkness—it was worse than bedlam let
loose.[11]

Under strain, nervous and hysterical women, says
Thomas L. Nichols, often fell senseless and rolled upon
the ground.[12] Then, writes James Flint, there would be
a wave of "shouting, screaming, clapping of hands,
leaping, jerking, falling, and swooning." [13] Should
someone feel the call to preach, he would climb up on a
stump, log, or wagon and hold forth. Richard McNemar
remembers such an incident:

A boy, from appearance about twelve years old, retired from the stand in time of preaching, under a very extraordinary impression; and having mounted a log, at some distance, and raising his voice, in a very affecting manner, he attracted the main body of the people, in a few minutes. With tears streaming from his eyes, he cried aloud to the wicked, warning them of their danger, denouncing their certain doom, if they persisted in their sins; expressing his love to their souls, and desire that they would turn to the Lord, and be saved. He was held up by two men, and spoke for about an hour, with that convincing eloquence that could be inspired only from above. When his strength seemed quite exhausted, and language failed to describe the feelings of his soul, he raised his hand, and dropping his handkerchief, wet with sweat from his little face, cried out: "Thus, O sinner! shall you drop into hell, unless you forsake your sins and turn to the Lord." [14]

Mourners would crowd down to the enclosure where a brigade of preachers and saints were kept busy praying for lost souls. Prodded by the "sisters" and "brothers" to surrender, a weeping and hysterical sinner reminded one sportsman of the cornered and exhausted wolf before the pack of hounds closed in for the kill. One wife was working so vigorously on her husband, pleading with him "to go to Jesus" and shaking him, that she maintained until her dying day that she actually felt the devil come out of him and enter their span of mules tied to a post-oak tree near the enclosure. The mules, her husband reported, almost broke their halters as they "cavorted and reared straight up" trying to get away, because they "felt on fire inside." In defense of such testimony, one preacher argued that a similar thing happened with Jesus in the country of the Gergesenes when he drove devils out of the two men from the tombs, into the herd of swine (Matt. 8:28–32). After three or four hours of this exciting and exhausting labor, there would be a benediction so that the people could get dinner, as well as recuperate.

Behind each tent one was apt to see fires burning, over which hung large, smoking pots containing savory food. Spiritual affairs were the main business of the day, but culinary interests were not neglected. After the meal there was a brief period for rest and, of course, for gossiping, a substitute for the newspaper in remote areas. Then there were prayer meetings in the various tents, and the more stubborn sinner again found himself the center of attraction. His popularity was proportional to the suspected sins. From the interior of the camp one sometimes could hear quite an assortment of noises—exhortations, prayers, and singing—coming from all quarters simultaneously. When more and more were converted, the shouting increased, the devil appeared literally to be pulled out of the mourners. The shouting then became joyful and triumphant—often as frenzied as that from sports enthusiasts when their team suddenly and unexpectedly wins. The devil, however, was handicapped in one of these protracted encounters because he was grossly outnumbered when the battle was fought around the altar instead of in the outskirts of the campgrounds, where his cohorts were entrenched.

After a lapse of time the horn would blow again to call everyone back to the clearing or the tabernacle, where a fresh preacher was waiting to resume the aggression against sin. Following a brief prayer and several "booming" hymns, he would signify his readiness to exhort by taking a drink of perhaps cool springwater out of a wooden bucket and gourd dipper that reposed by the pulpit. Many were usually still staggering under the struggle of the morning, hardly conscious that the preacher was talking; the blackness of their sins and the fiery billows of hell loomed up before them so threateningly that they were nearing the breaking point. They could virtually feel their souls frying. Even the calmest and most rational person had difficulty maintaining his equilibrium when all about him were those with such unsettled emotions. As a rule, those recording the ecstatic behavior attempted realism, and in so doing, they often painted unconsciously some rather ludicrous pictures. James Flint writes:

> A most pathetic prayer was poured forth, and a profound silence reigned over all the camp, except the fenced enclosure, from whence a low hollow murmuring sound issued. Now and then *Amen* was articulated in a pitiful and indistinct tone of voice. You have seen a menagerie of wild animals on a journey, and have perhaps heard the king of beasts, and other powerful quadrupeds, excited to grumbling by the jolting of the wagon. Probably you will call this a rude simile: but it is the most accurate that I can think of.[15]

Bedlam was more concentrated in the enclosures for the mourners. Chaos predominated here with so many simultaneously trying to "pray through." When the individual succeeded in unburdening himself of his sins, the effect was like an electric shock. He might signify his joy and relief by shouting and jumping into the air. Besides these mourners, there were the small groups praying for the more stubborn sinners.

The night meeting, climaxing a series of activities, saw some of the most unusual phenomena, for all during the day those under conviction worked slowly up to the height of their emotional experience, which frequently came at this culminating service. After the evening meal, the camp was lighted with the lanterns from trees and the many fires of pine knots. The lights would shine in the tents and gleam in the forest. It was a scene that seemed, to one observer, wild and beautiful. The ringing of Methodist hymns through the woods, the rays of the moon on the tree tops, the melancholy scream of the loon, the cry of the waterfowl from across the lake (as one poetic soul observed), the powerful voice of the preacher, and the spectacle of march-

ing men and women singing their pleas to sinners—all
presented a background for a rich harvest of converts.
The torchlight processions at night were also remarkable spectacles, and even the stoutest sinner could
hardly resist as they marched and sang:

> "Sinners, will you scorn the Savior?
> Will you drive Him from your arms?
> Once He died for your behavior,
> Now He calls you to His charms."

If such pleading did not bring him to the anxious
seats, then the thrilling optimism of that "tumultuous
chorus" was sure to stir the emotions:

> "I am bound for the Kingdom!
> Will you go to Glory with me?
> O Hallelujah! O Halle-hallelujah!
> I am bound for the Kingdom!
> Will you go to Glory with me?
> O Hallelujah! O praise ye the Lord!" [16]

Services were known to last all night, as James Flint
recalls: "At half past two A.M. I got into a tent, stretched
myself on the ground, and was soon lulled asleep by
the music. About five I was awakened by the unceasing
melody." [17] Of course, most of the people would retire
to their tents, where groups would continue in prayer
for the more rugged of the unconverted. Often the "seekers" would break under the intense pressure from the
pleading of loved ones and friends. In the better-
organized meetings the horn would sound about ten
o'clock to end the activities of the first day, but the altar
service could continue until daybreak. For sometimes,
as the antebellum preachers liked to say, a Jacob would
wrestle with his "angel" all night before at last "pin-
ning his shoulders down."

Some of the strangest phenomena recorded in our
religious history occurred at camp meetings. In the

height of frenzy, certain evidences of animal feeling were made manifest. Certainly there was a little deception, but by and large these experiences were genuine. For example, on one occasion John Lyle recorded in his diary that, suspecting humbug, he applied a vial of hartshorn to a stout young man's nostrils while he was lying on his back, but the man was so absorbed by devotional feeling that he did not notice the discomfort.

At the outset one will be apt to doubt these emotional orgies, but when forty or fifty reliable observers concur in their testimonies, he will become more hospitable to what at first seem like only cock-and-bull stories or "old wives' tales." "Bodily exercises," as they were called, are extremely important for the light they throw on the nature of Southern religion in these early days. The fact that similar behavior has been reported in present-day services is even more significant; some of this older emotionalism has endured and now finds expression in a variety of manifestations. Very often contemporaries tried to generalize about denominations on the basis of outlandish behavior. James Flint, for instance, writes:

> I should be sorry to abuse the Methodist sect by the illiberal application of such terms as fanaticism, superstition, or illusion. I have known many of them who are valuable members of society, and several who have rendered important services to their country, but have not seen anyone prostrated, or even visibly affected, at the camp-meeting or elsewhere, whom I know to be men of strong minds or of much intelligence. Females seem to be more susceptible of the impressions than men are. A quality perhaps that is to be imputed to the greater sensibility of their feelings.[18]

Generalizations like Flint's, of course, are dangerous, but by far the majority of rural people attending were mercurial and volatile. However, at a camp meeting the caste system was apt to be demolished. Episcopalians,

Presbyterians, Baptists, and Methodists, cultured and vulgar, rich and poor—all were known to be in the same enclosure, irrational with religious feeling.

Excitement such as this was not unusual even on the college campuses of the Old South. In many instances, however, revivals may have had their beginnings off the campuses, perhaps over a weekend or between sessions when students came in contact with spiritual activity in their respective communities. Revivals might start spontaneously among the students themselves or could even be motivated by faculty or ministerial candidates. Albea Godbold, in *The Church College of the Old South,* has reported thirty-eight revivals in educational institutions of the Old South, distributed among the denominations as follows: Methodists, 18; Baptists, 14; Presbyterians, 4; and Episcopalians, 2. The "Second Great Awakening" received some of its impetus from two such campus revivals at Hampden-Sydney and Washington, both in Virginia.[19] Some of the trained leadership of the evangelical movement came from such religious experiences on the campus, but the lay preacher was the most important force in the whole movement. There may have been less evidence of sheer animalism among students, but occasionally a president would have to advise against excessive shouting, jumping, and prostration. The emotion might become so intense at times that the routine of a college program would have to be suspended. Student diaries reveal that the young, being extremely concerned about the status of their souls, were thoroughly captivated by this Southern type of evangelicalism.

"Bodily exercises" were familiarly known at the time, and included "falling," "jerking," "rolling," "running," "dancing," "barking," "laughing," "singing," and having "visions" and "trances."

Perhaps the earliest instances of the "falling exercise" occurred at Red River, Kentucky, in 1799, in

McGready's church during the preaching of John McGee. Like an epidemic it spread through Tennessee, upper Kentucky, and into the Carolinas. "The word of God," writes Gallaher, "was quick and powerful, and sharper than any two-edged sword, piercing even to the dividing asunder of the soul and spirit, and of the joints and marrow." [20] During fiery preaching or spirited and lively singing—when their bodies were exhausted from copious weeping—strong men, businessmen, and unemotional men would suddenly fall prostrate on the ground and swoon away. Male and female, old and young, robust and frail—all were subject to the "workings of the Spirit." Barton Stone, until 1803 an evangelical Presbyterian, says, "The falling exercise was very common among all classes, the saints and sinners of every age and of every grade, from the philosopher to the clown." [21] One would pitch forward as if struck by lightning; he might shake violently the moment before; or he might shriek before falling. And occasionally as the victim lay on the ground he would groan and beg for mercy. Most generally, however, the subject would "with a piercing scream fall like a log on the floor, earth, or mud, and appear as dead." [22] Stone recalls such an instance:

> At a meeting, two gay young ladies, sisters, were standing together attending to the exercises and preaching at the time. Instantly they both fell, with a shriek of distress, and lay for more than an hour apparently in a lifeless state. . . . After awhile, the gloom on the face of one was succeeded by a heavenly smile, and she cried out, precious Jesus, and rose up and spoke of the love of God.[23]

Robert Davidson recalled that often an individual would receive some forewarning by the approach of a pricking sensation—a feeling of numbness in the body.[24] After he had fallen once, he was likely to fall again from exhaustion. Women were known to drop from their horses onto the road and lie sometimes from fifteen minutes to two or three hours before recovering. One woman lay for nine days and nights without eating or speaking.[25] When the subjects regained consciousness, they would generally shout and sing for joy.

Several contemporaries described the physical reaction of a mortal while under such a strange spell. Lyle, for example, has reported that sometimes the pulse was higher and faster than usual. For instance, one woman who had been shouting and preaching madly had the veins in her neck become quite enlarged, and another "had her breast to become swollen considerably." The face was usually pale or a pale yellow like that of a corpse, or it might even be a faint red. Frequently the breathing was hard and strained. Some victims were completely relaxed and limp, while others were so taut and cramped that the hands would have to be pried open.[26] If the creature was not completely motionless, he might resemble a small child having a tantrum, kicking his heels and bouncing the back of his head against the floor. Truly these were religious convulsions.

When one pitched forward thus, Gallaher reports members of the congregation as saying to themselves: "Here was the avowed infidel, prostrate on the ground, confessing and lamenting his folly before God. There was the notorious profligate, crying for mercy. Here was the celebrated frontier warrior. . . . And there was the humbled politician. . . ." [27] Apparently those harboring some guilt or sin were more apt to be affected by this and other religious exercises than were the pious.

At the Cabin Creek camp meeting, May 22, 1801, according to Davidson, so many fell on the third night that the converts were collected and laid out like dead bodies in a safe place. Two hundred fell at the Paint Creek sacrament; three hundred fell at Pleasant Point; three thousand fell at Cane Ridge on August 6, 1801.[28] Peter Cartwright reports that five hundred fell in one of his meetings. Finley states that he saw about five hundred swept down instantaneously as though a thousand big guns had been turned on them.

Most disturbing of all were the "jerks," affecting one as though he were touched repeatedly on various parts of the body with a hot iron or a live electrical wire. The exercise, McNemar believed, usually began in the head, causing it to fly backward and forward, from side to side, with a quick jolt.[29] Forked lightning seemed to leap from head to head, and wild thunder to hover over the large assemblies. The ruin of vanity and fine clothes, this religious spasm amused Methodist preachers. In his *Autobiography*, Peter Cartwright says:

> To see those proud young gentlemen and young ladies dressed in their silks, jewelry, and prunella, from top to toe, take the jerks, would often excite my risibilities. The first jerk or so, you would see their fine bonnets, caps, and combs fly; and so sudden would be the jerking of the head that their long loose hair would crack almost as loud as a wagoner's whip.[30]

Similarly, Jo C. Guild recalls that in the early days beautiful women had long black hair, some auburn, others red, with different shades of color. They wore it plaited, forming a crescent around the head; and, he adds, "when the stream of eloquence copiously flowed over the large assembly, when all the fires were lit up, I have heard this plaited hair pop like the crack of a wagon whip." [31] He had seen as many as a hundred women jerking from religious enthusiasm. The more one tried to control himself, the more he twitched. Cartwright remembers how a drunkard became affected in trying to disturb a camp meeting:

> He halted among some saplings, and although he was violently agitated, he took out his bottle of whiskey, and swore he would drink the damned jerks to death; but he jerked at such a rate he could not get the bottle to his

mouth, though he tried hard. At length he fetched a sudden jerk, and the bottle struck a sapling and was broken
to pieces, and spilled his whiskey on the ground. There
was a great crowd gathered round him, and when he lost
his whiskey he became very much enraged, and cursed
and swore very profanely, his jerks still increasing. At
length he fetched a very violent jerk, snapped his neck,
fell, and soon expired, with his mouth full of cursing and
bitterness.[32]

Sometimes one's features would be so distorted, observed McNemar, that the appearance would completely change, and the head would twitch right and
left until the face appeared as much behind as before. A
handkerchief bound tightly about the head would be
thrown off with the very first twitch.[33] Some were
known to stand in one place and jerk backward and
forward in quick succession, the head almost touching
the ground before and behind. So violent became the
jerking at times that fears were awakened lest the poor
mortal might dash out his brains or snap his neck, as
some had done.

One could even be taken with the "jerks" at his work
or in his home. T. C. Anderson in his *Life of Rev.
George Donnell* recalls an incident of a venerable
clergyman who was spending the night with a friend
following a preaching service. The old man's mind
began to dwell on the pleasant thoughts of the presence, holiness, and majesty of God when he suddenly
felt that he would be overawed by the Holy Spirit. In
trying to find solitude he crossed a cornfield; then in-
voluntarily he "began leaping about, first forward, then
sidewise, and sometimes, standing still, he would
swing backward and forward, see-saw fashion." His
friends came running to his assistance and with difficulty carried him into the house, where an hour
elapsed before the paroxysm passed. But the next day
while he was talking with a friend about the meeting
"he was suddenly seized again and jerked across the

room, and continued under the influence of the exercise about fifteen minutes." [34]

McGready tells a similar story of one who began jerking in his own room. A young man, the son of an elder in the church, pretended to be ill one Sabbath in order to escape going to camp meeting. So he went to bed, where he planned to remain until his parents were out of sight. His thoughts all the while were directed to the service as he visualized the multitude, the worship, and the bodily exercises. Suddenly he was jerked out of bed, dashed around the room, and against the walls. Remembering that prayer was a good sedative, he fell on his knees to quell the attack. Going back to his bed to rest a few minutes, he was stricken again. Finally he dressed and went out to the tanyard to work, but when he grasped a knife it was flirted out of his hand. This time he was hurled backward over logs and against fences as if by an invisible assailant. At last he returned to his room, where he prayed in dead earnestness, weeping and crying for mercy. Here his parents found him when they returned.[35]

Behavior like this was more than Lorenzo Dow, the eccentric circuit preacher, could accept, but his skepticism was short-lived. He recalls the experiences that convinced him that the jerks were authentic:

> I passed by a meeting-house, where I observed the undergrowth had been cut up for a camp-meeting, and from fifty to one hundred saplings left breast high, which to me appeared so slovenish that I could not but ask my guide the cause, who observed they were topped so high, and left for the people to jerk by. This so excited my attention that I went over the ground to view it; and found where the people had laid hold of them and jerked so powerfully that they had kicked up the earth as a horse stamping flies.[36]

He found further proof in one of his meetings where he saw many jerking irresistibly. A Presbyterian minister whom he trusted told him about an incident he had witnessed where a young man from North Carolina, while mimicking those who were jerking, became likewise affected. Growing ashamed, he attempted to mount his horse to ride away, but "his foot jerked about so that he could not put it into the stirrup; some youngsters seeing this, assisted him on, but he jerked so that he could not sit alone, and one got up to hold him on, which was done with difficulty." [37] Becoming increasingly interested in the strange phenomena, Dow observed that when the subject did not resist, he experienced no bodily pain, but that when he fought against the attack, he suffered a deadness and barrenness over the mind. Onlookers have noted that when the subject yielded to the attack, he often became happy, a heavenly smile and solemnity appearing on the countenance. Those who began jerking were instructed not to resist but to let the "Holy Spirit have its way." When one submitted thus, the eyes reflected an inner transformation; they would be fixed upon an invisible object above, an image that only the true Christian was supposed to comprehend.

People today can hardly be expected to accept an extravaganza like the "jerks." Anticipating doubt, T. Marshall Smith, a historian of the post-Revolutionary period, tries to assure his readers of the authenticity of the strange phenomena that occurred in the McGee meetings. He states that he relied "upon the statements of hundreds of eye-witnesses of the events themselves, the contemporaries and intimate acquaintances and friends of the Messrs. McGee, whose lives of piety and usefulness they well knew from the beginning."

The rolling exercise consisted of one's being hurled down violently, doubled with the head and feet together, and rolled over and over like a wheel. Or the person might fall prostrate, testified McNemar, and be rolled over and over like a log.[38] Such behavior might seem ludicrous to the onlooker, particularly when a vain lady of society, adorned in all the finery of her class, would roll insensibly through mud or water. Struggling sinners, however, were unconscious of natural obstacles when under the influence of a spiritual anesthetic.

The running exercise was full of dangers, because the victim often behaved like a cat or dog having a fit, or he might start up and dash away as though at the beginning of a footrace. Benches, fences, wagons, and streams were no obstacles at all. Insensitive to pain, he might run against first one barrier and then another, frequently falling from fatigue or collision with a solid object. Lyle recalls seeing a woman fall and lie motionless for some time; then suddenly she wanted "to serve God." She was, stated McNemar, so beside herself with emotion that her friends tried in vain to hold her. She climbed first over one bench and then another until she fell again. According to John Rogers, Barton Stone knew a young physician of a distinguished family who came from a great distance to observe the peculiar camp-meeting behavior. He and a young lady had jokingly agreed to take care of one another if either should become affected and fall. But strange to say, after a time he began to feel numb, and from sheer fright turned to run from the congregation into the woods. He did not get very far, however, before he fell, and there he lay until he was converted.[39]

The dancing exercise, both voluntary and involuntary, came to be a more refined feature of the revival meeting. The former type could be stopped at the will of the participant; whereas the latter, perhaps originally motivated by the subject but overpowering him, could not be checked. It became the most common type of dance. Leaping and skipping was a good indication that sinners had suddenly been relieved of their burdens and had "made peace with God." They wanted the world to see "the holy child" in them. The schismatics condoned dancing, says McNemar, for they felt that this expression of great joy marked an improvement, growth, and advancement in the spirit of the revival.[40] Some antebellum religionists included the exercise of voluntary dancing as a part of the church worship; for example, a Brother Thompson in the spring sacrament at Turtle Creek (1804) set the precedent. At the close of his service he would begin dancing and continue for as long as an hour, repeating in a low voice, "This is the Holy Ghost—Glory!" [41]

That a denomination publicly sanctioned dancing as a method of praising God and making merry is hardly true. Only smaller dissenting groups made a general practice of authorizing such unusual conduct. However, it occasionally broke out in camp meetings. A contributor to the *Biblical Repertory* recalls that he saw a woman become overjoyed in a Presbyterian service during the administration of the Lord's Supper, in the presence of the Synod of Virginia. Her pew was cleared to give her plenty of room, and she danced for half an hour, with eyes closed and calm countenance. Finally she fell and became afflicted with other motions.[42]

Another extravagance was called the "barks," commonly considered an affliction sent not upon the blasphemous and depraved alone but upon the vain as well. It had its origin, reputedly, in eastern Tennessee at the expense of an old Presbyterian preacher. He had gone into the woods, mused Rogers, for private devotion when he was seized with the jerks, and clutching a sapling to keep from falling, he uttered a grunt or noise similar to a bark, with his face turned upward. Someone found him in this position and spread the report that the old fellow was barking up a tree.[43] David Benedict remarked that it was a common thing to hear people barking just like a pack of spaniels. He says, "They would start up suddenly in a fit of barking, rush out, roam around, and in a short time come barking and foaming back." [44] Down on all fours they sometimes went, growling, snapping their teeth, and barking just like dogs. There was no rescue, except perhaps in the voluntary dance; only a full confession of one's sins and a complete submission to God's will, according to the preachers, would bring relief. People were afraid to ridicule or doubt lest they be stricken in a similar fashion. Davidson writes thus:

> Ludicrous as it may now seem to us, at this distance of time, to hear of such extraordinary sounds as "bow, wow, wow," interspersed with pious ejaculations, and quotations of Scripture, as "every knee shall bow-wow-wow, and every tongue shall confess," we are not at liberty to doubt the truth of the assertion that then the effect, or at least one of the effects, was to overawe the wicked, and excite fearful apprehensions in the minds of the impious.[45]

The laughing exercise was common. It amounted to a loud, hearty laughter, which was not contagious. The person was rapturously solemn, his deportment commanding the utmost respect from the religious.[46] However, it came to be exaggerated, the congregation often laughing aloud at the conclusion of certain sentences. In short, the "Holy Laugh" may remind some of the less-sophisticated Negro's "Yea, man," and the "Amen" of rural Methodists, or of certain minor sects that have given services an atmosphere of informality. In the hands of rowdies the sanctioned laughter could become detrimental to a worshipful atmosphere, for what preacher could detect a spurious exhibition of holy zeal?

The singing exercise was indeed a strange phenomenon, primarily because the subject sang not from his mouth or nose, but from his breast. When this music began, all else often ceased, so peculiar was the freakish spectacle. Barton Stone and J. B. Campbell were sitting near a pious lady who began exercising thus.

They described the sound as heavenly and surpassing anything they had ever known in nature.[47]

Those who fell or swooned were known at times to remain insensible for hours. During periods of unconsciousness the persons were very often favored with visions. Heavenly singing, interviews with the spirits of departed dead, visions of two suns or three moons, a purgatorial fire, flocks of ravenous birds, a track of light a thousand miles in length, the crossing of rivers and climbing of mountains, finding treasure, fighting serpents, eating the fruit of the tree of knowledge, bathing in pellucid streams, and exchanging old garments for new—these are some of the threads out of which visions were spun. Interesting are some of the incidents cited by Davidson from the Diary of John Lyle, who observed at Lexington in October 1801:

H. McD.'s wife fell, and swooned away; thought, when she came to, she had been asleep. Dreamt she was walking on the tops of the trees. . . . K. C. swoons often; and in one swoon saw a vision of heaven, with a small door. J. C. is in despair; had had a vision of hell, and heard a voice saying, that he must die without religion in such a time. . . . One W. was much agitated, and talked a good deal about sin and Christ, and exhorted and prayed. That night, slumbering, or as he thought, wide awake, his spirit went out (as in a trance, I suppose) into the earth, and saw strange, curious caverns, &c., and then he thought he would look upwards, and he saw a mountain clothed with beautiful trees, silver-topped, or leaves tipped with silver. He thought this mountain led to God and heaven. Then above he saw a great light, and he prayed to see a little farther; and a little to the right he saw still more dazzling light, and he sighed and sunk before it, as the great All in all. He came to tell of these things in ecstasies of joy, and appeared very thankful for the great view. I inquired if he had any view of anything but light. He said, nothing but dazzling light, such as he could not behold; and he thought it was the place where God dwelt, &c. . . . Two women in Stonermouth have fallen into trances, (July 12, 1801) and one has passed a golden bridge to heaven's gate, &c. The other has been in heaven, &c.[48]

The camp meetings and revivalism, with all the accompanying techniques and weird manifestations, left an imprint upon the religion of the entire section. The religion revealed emotional rather than rational qualities; in many instances charges of immorality were brought against some who were overcome by their feelings and those who exploited the gullible. Perhaps today some may conclude that it was more concerned with putting man into heaven than heaven into man; but in the South the religionists' concern with a social gospel was not forthcoming until the twentieth century. There was a preoccupation with salvation from personal sin and a yearning for the life hereafter, but such an emphasis made the religion no less popular or influential, as contemporaries seemed to indicate.

Numerous writers during the period agree with Spencer when he states that the revival of 1800 was one of the most wonderful events of modern time. It seemed to him more like the instantaneous conversion of a nation than the regeneration of a few individuals. He says:

If a traveller had passed through the whole breadth of the settled portions of North America, in 1799, he would have heard the songs of the drunkard, the loud swearing and obscenity of crowds around taverns, and the bold, blasphemous vaunting of infidels, in every village and hamlet. If he had returned in 1801, he would have heard, instead, the proclamation of the gospel to awed multitudes, earnest prayers in the groves and forests, and songs of praise to God, along all the public thoroughfares.[49]

A. W. Putnam writes that as early as 1788 church leaders in Tennessee saw a day of religious frenzy approaching. The general feeling, he says, was that the re-

vival was really a blessing in spite of its faults. "Better
so, a thousand times better so, than heartless infidelity,
or to have yielded to any debasing idolatry or hurtful
superstition." For after the strange and anomalous conditions passed away, there was a general improvement,
exemplified by the careful study of "the word of God,"
much exhortation and prayer, and the advancement of
useful knowledge and good morals. His figure of a
storm is appropriate:

> There was a tornado: it overthrew many a tall Anakim, it
> cast down some of the haughty ones, and exalted too
> highly some men of low degree. A few mighty oaks were
> topped or prostrated, and gave space for sun and air and
> genial rains. A thousand blooming shrubs and the thick
> waving harvest, and doubtless some rank weeds, have
> found room to flourish. It was strange work; but it was
> one of the ways of Providence.[50]

The fact that the vast majority of those who professed
religion lived better lives thereafter and that "scoffing
infidelity" was silenced testified to the contemporary
that revivalism had its effect. A typical estimate is made
by T. C. Anderson when he states that wherever revivalism was felt "public morals were reformed, infidelity
was silenced, religion was respected, the house of God
crowded with attentive and devout worshippers, thousands were converted, and Christians rendered more
conscientious in duty and more spiritual in devotion." [51] Churches were strengthened, new ones were
organized, ministers preached with more zeal, and new
men were "called of God." A survey published in the
View of the United States of America reveals that religion was gaining ground by 1820, a trend that continued
throughout the pre–Civil War period:

> That cold-blooded compound of irreligion, irony, selfish-
> ness, and sarcasm, formerly so prevalent, is by no means
> common at present; which is a strong proof of the exis-

tence of a great mass of real piety in the country. Another convincing proof of the increase of religion is the rapid spread of Sunday schools, and of missionary and Bible societies.[52]

Ignorance, poverty, and vice in the larger cities had diminished. The Sabbath came to be respected by all. Ladies and gentlemen of the most respectable families without hesitation taught the Sunday scholars—Negro and white, old and young. Certainly revivalism and camp meetings played a part in giving the section its characteristic religiousness and the subsequent title of "the Bible Belt," the term of twentieth-century origin.

Although the phenomenon of revivalism was not restricted to the South, it did have greater popularity there than elsewhere. It was particularly popular with (among others) yeoman farmers, Negroes, and the so-called squatters (later, "sharecroppers" and "poor whites"), with whom the South was so generously endowed. Before the Civil War the revival, then, on a wide and far-reaching scale was identified more with the upper and lower South and the old Southwest than it was with any other section of the country. The camp meeting helped pattern the religious culture, becoming one outlet for pent-up emotion. For rural folk it was their summer picnic or fall festival after the crops were readied or gathered, or the land was laid by. Hence revivalism, as manifested in the camp meeting, with all its techniques, undoubtedly exercised considerable influence upon Southern religious behavior and thought, reducing theological discussion, intellectual considerations, and interest in social issues. A simple, unacademic, and emotional type of faith was firmly fixed. According to Charles A. Johnson in his book on frontier religion, the camp meeting might even be blamed for having "introduced a strong flavor of intolerance into the lives of the plain people of the South." [53]

4

The Man in the Pulpit

IN PERIODS of economic and political crisis America has produced sufficient leaders. For example, men like Washington, Franklin, Hamilton, Jefferson, and Lincoln, who now transcend controversy, have left indelible imprints upon the minds of hero-worshipers and upon the structure of our government. When Southerners search through their special archives for those who have guided them in moments of indecision, they will find their pilots too. In the area of Protestant religion, for instance, each group contributed its leaders: the Methodists, their traveling "firebrands" or "sons of thunder" who rode a regular circuit; the Baptists, their farmer preachers who on weekends went where they were called; the Presbyterians and Episcopalians, their settled clergy who served designated congregations or parishes; and the Disciples, their lay volunteers who followed the settlers as they moved into the Mississippi Valley.

The preachers who exerted the greatest influence upon the cultural and social life of the Southern section were the circuit riders and farmer preachers. These gospel missionaries, as they went proselyting through the wilderness, indoctrinated the agrarian mind with a denominational orthodoxy (an unshakable loyalty to a particular sect), which often contributed to dividing religionists into warring groups. The better-educated ministers, generally Presbyterian and Episcopalian, perfected in their college classrooms or sanctuaries a theological orthodoxy which gave substance to a great deal of the religious controversy that characterized the Old South.

However, the type of preacher most instrumental in the development of the social and intellectual life of the times was neither the aristocratic Episcopalian, with his pomp and his apostolic succession, nor the Presbyterian Bourbon, with his taste for theology and culture, but one of the common people, generally a Methodist or a Baptist by confession. He was an ordinary apostle to the poor—an unlettered gentleman, in the broad sense, and a good shepherd, like Chaucer's "poor parson," whose sheep were scattered sometimes over an area of one hundred square miles. He was usually of the lower class; however, such a status was really an asset. Understanding the habits, feelings, and prejudices of the frontier mind, he could adapt to the intellectual level and the mores of the common people, to become familiar with their personal and family problems. He was very frequently a father confessor. Thus his usefulness to community and church was increased because of this humble birth and simple way of life. Through the confidence which the people gained from his great sympathy and compassion he was able to make an orthodox faith palatable and intelligible to them all. He was instrumental in bringing about a fusion of piety with everyday pursuits and even with the innocent amusements of life. As Thomas Hamilton (perhaps facetiously) observed in his travels through the South, young ladies came to chant hymns instead of Irish melodies, and the "profane chorus" gave way to "rhythmical Doxologies." "Grog parties commenced with prayer, and terminate[d] with benediction. Devout smokers [said] grace over a cigar, and chewers of the

Nicotin weed [inserted] a fresh quid with an expression of pious gratitude." [1]

Quite likely this "son of thunder" followed some trade—most often followed the plow—before answering the call to preach. His ministerial diploma was from nature. Yet he was perhaps the best-informed man along the frontier—a versatile conversationalist on politics, religion, nature, farming, and hunting, and eloquent in his interpretation of the divine. Above all, he knew people. He learned to know them in the evening by the fireside; he exchanged tall tales with them at the country stores, and shouldered arms with them in their common battle against the devil. These Methodist warriors were members of a team; perhaps in the more thickly populated areas they assisted a located preacher, a Sunday school teacher, or an exhorter. But for many years they were the only messengers of the gospel along the frontier, daily on the move and subject to rotation at least every two years. By 1849, notes Charles A. Johnson, the Methodists in the old Southwest (the Deep South of today) had 1,476 itinerants as compared to 3,026 located ministers. [2]

A prejudice developed very early against salaried or "hireling preachers." Not only did the populace cry out about the practice of paying ministers but also some preachers themselves spoke with feeling on the matter. For example, Alexander Campbell, before his departure from the fellowship of the Baptists, spoke vigorously against "hireling preachers." Methodists, however, in spite of public sentiment, felt the practical need to give their circuit riders a small stipend, yet hardly enough to keep body and soul together. So it became necessary for many of the itinerants to provide for their temporal necessities by secular employment. This state of affairs frequently had a bad effect upon the pulpit, since lay ministers often found little time to study. As reported by Spencer, as late as 1835 the church historian William C. Buck wrote about the Baptist leadership:

Often did the preacher plow with the only horse he pos-
sessed, five days in the week, and Saturday morning til
10 o'clock, then ride the jaded animal to meeting, enter
the pulpit, physically, and mentally wearied and wor-
ried, and attempt to preach to the people assembled,
without having spent one hour in preparing for the solemn duty.[3]

The picture in the Methodist Church for many years
was almost as gloomy. David Ramsey states that in
1785, the Methodists of South Carolina spent as little as
$2,080 on 17,784 sermons, or about 12 cents per ser-
mon.[4] William Warren Sweet writes that before 1800
the circuit rider's annual income was $64 plus a travel-
ing allowance. The following year the fixed salary was
$80; in 1816, $100.[5] Peter Cartwright states that nine
out of ten never received more than half the designated
sum and estimates that in fifty-three years of preaching,
he had a net loss of $6,400; however, the personal satis-
faction in having helped to revitalize spiritually a great
mass of people more than compensated for any material
losses.[6] Too, he expected a generous reward "up yon-
der," where he hoped to settle down and rest for a long,
long time.

In the early days, when a man felt the call to preach
he did not inquire for the best college or seminary; instead, says Cartwright, he

hunted up a hardy pony of a horse, and some traveling
apparatus, and with his library always at hand, namely,
Bible, Hymn-Book, and Discipline, he started, and with
a text that never wore out nor grew stale, he cried, "Behold the Lamb of God, that taketh away the sins of the
world." In this way he went through storms of wind,
hail, snow, and rain; climbed hills and mountains, traversed valleys, plunged through swamps, swam swollen
streams, lay out all night, wet, weary, and hungry, held
his horse by the bridle all night, or tied him to a limb,
slept with his saddle blanket for a bed, his saddle or
saddle-bags for his pillow, and his old big coat or blan-

ket, if he had any, for a covering. Often he slept in dirty cabins, on earthen floors, before the fire; ate roasting ears for bread, drank buttermilk for coffee, or sage tea for imperial; took, with a hearty zest, deer or bear meat, or wild turkey, for breakfast, dinner, and supper, if he could get it. His text was always ready, "Behold the Lamb of God." [7]

Here we see the life of the itinerant Baptist, Methodist, and Disciples of Christ preachers. Cartwright wonders, in looking back upon the experiences and hardships of other days, whether or not under such circumstances now there would be many to say, "Here am I, Lord, send me."

Life seemed long to the itinerant, alone so much of the time in sparsely settled country. He spent days in the saddle, nights very often in the open air under the stars. There was little variety of scenes and events between appointments.

His frame and weather-beaten visage usually revealed the adversity of travel. Starvation, swamps, alligators, Indians, highway robbers, rowdies, bilious fevers, and exposure to the elements—all these obstacles taxed his endurance and checked the progress of the gospel in the wilderness. But he was rarely beaten or discouraged for long because he believed firmly in the wisdom and power of the Deity.

Of the trials and sometimes ordeals that preachers had to undergo, their memoirs are profuse with illustration. The Baptist historian James Spencer records that in 1778 David Barrow, accompanied by a minister named Mintz, was invited to preach at the house of a gentleman living on the Nansemond River, near the mouth of the James. The two of them had not gone far on their journey when they were informed that they could expect trouble if they tried to bring their spurious Baptist doctrine into the community. A group of rowdies attended the service and dragged the ministers from the pulpit, giving them such a prolonged baptizing in a hole of water nearby that Barrow was almost drowned. The story continues, though, in a characteristic vein, revealing that several of the rowdies died miserable deaths only a few weeks later.[8]

The experiences of William H. Raper, as reported by W. H. Venable, are typical of the Southerner's faith. During his travels he traversed virgin forests, swam rivers, and encamped all night in the midst of turbulent rain or snowstorm, with only the heavens and the branches of a tree for cover. One night he was lost in the woods and had been wandering around for hours. He came to a swollen stream which separated him from shelter on the other side. Dismounting and groping his way along in the darkness, he came to what he thought was a battered and flimsy bridge. With considerable effort he dragged his horse across and reached the hospitable quarters awaiting him. The next morning, after revealing to his friends his ordeal, Raper discovered that in the darkness he had crossed on floating driftwood that had become jammed. This narrow escape gave him even greater confidence in the guiding hand of Providence, to which he attributed his deliverance from the flood.

On another occasion Raper was trying to ford a raging stream when his horse threw him. The swift current rendered him helpless, but he managed to grasp an overhanging branch. At the moment when he was about to surrender to the water, his strength gone, he thought he heard his mother's voice praying for him. Then with hope renewed, he struggled to the bank, and a few days later he learned that his mother had actually been praying at the very hour when he supposedly recognized her voice.[9] This was the type of faith that kept the itinerant going during the early days. It was likewise the kind of faith that guided the South in its formative years.

Horse, rifle, saddlebag, a change of clothes, the Bible, a copy of Charles Wesley's or Isaac Watts's hymns, a

volume of John Wesley's sermons (if he was a Methodist), and a bite of bread: here we find the equipment for
a traveling preacher in the old days. He began his ministry before there were railways, telegraph, and sometimes even roads; communication was in its earliest
stages. In the early morning, upon leaving a humble
cabin where he may have been plagued by filth and
fleas, he would inquire about his course to the next
house or community. Like the mariner on uncharted
seas, he relied upon the stars or a compass to direct him
through forests and miry swamps, over hills and dales,
and over unbridged streams to a group of people—
sometimes only two or three families—waiting to hear
his plan for their salvation.

Although his novel *The Circuit Rider: A Tale of the
Heroic Age* has its setting in Indiana, Edward Eggleston frequently relies on parental accounts of experiences along the Southern frontier. He gives a realistic
picture of the cordial reception extended the preacher.
Next to a house-raising, the camp meeting, a wedding,
Christmas, or "hog-killing," his coming was one of the
major events. His arrival attracted the attention of all,
from master to vicious mongrels. Colonel Wheeler, after
fighting the dogs off the horseman, asked his guest to
dismount. Learning the news from one of the children,
Mrs. Wheeler hurried to wash her hands, for she had not
been given a "good-old-fashioned Methodist shake-
hands," she said, since leaving Pittsburgh. In custom-
ary fashion the Colonel opened his home to be used for
preaching services, sending word to his neighbors in
the village. However, there were those in the community who were not altogether hospitable. Something of
the prejudice of the times is revealed in a comment by
one of the people:

> "Laws-a-massy! You don' say! A Methodist? One of the
> shoutin' kind, that knocks folks down when he preaches!
> What will the Captain [Lumsden] do? They do say he

does hate the Methodis' worse nar copperhead snakes, now. Some old quarrel, liker'n not. Well, I'm goin' jist to see how redikl'us Methodis' does do!" [10]

Lumsden promptly planned a dance in conflict with Magruder's meeting, but this type of Presbyterian opposition, not necessarily typical of every community, could not forestall what was destined to occur. An evangelical religion like Methodism was bound to be popular among a people made lethargic by the warm Southern sun and the monotonous toil on the farm. It supplied the less sophisticated, the ignorant, and the uninhibited with a petcock for the release of emotion and also an opportunity for friends to meet socially. The preaching services gave a much-needed escape from planting, harvesting, and plowing. Also, such a religion was simple and practical.

The new evangelical religion was, indeed, suited to the people's needs and temperament. Neither individual prejudice nor collective opposition could check the revivalistic movement when it had champions like Eggleston's Magruder, a man with physical as well as spiritual strength. His broad shoulders, powerful arms, shaggy brows, and coarse features revealed that he was a seasoned warrior, who had perhaps been a blacksmith before becoming a circuit rider. His masculinity won the respect of rural people. His bellowing voice shook the Colonel's cabin windows; surely he was a "son of thunder." "He prayed as a man talking face to face with the Almighty Judge of the generation of men; he prayed with an undoubting assurance of his own acceptance with God, and with the sincerest conviction of the infinite peril of his unforgiven hearers." [11] Preachers like Magruder perhaps lacked the refinement of the Mathers and Jonathan Edwards of New England; yet they had what the South expected and appreciated more than culture and learning; they had conviction. "One Tishbite Elijah, that can thunder out of a heart that never doubts," says Eggleston, "is worth a thousand acute writers of ingenious apologies."

Conviction and emotional might, however, as students of homiletics know, do not ensure quality. A. De Puy Van Buren, a schoolmistress visiting for a year in the South, had an opportunity to hear many of these Methodist "Boanerges." One in particular remained in her memory because of the empty thought and great noise.

> I lost the text in the low-voice in which it was announced, and I lost most of the sermon in the loud-voice in which it was delivered. The little snow-ball that started at the top of the hill, came down upon us, at the foot, in perfect avalanche. I could not help thinking that this man had enough material in him to make two or three common ministers.[12]

The natives, though, thrived on this kind of Sunday fare.

Although many pulpiteers were only raw recruits, they knew how to utilize the folk conception of hell and the Day of Judgment. Their heaven was an inducement to living the good life, their hell was enough to frighten the wayward. The poet T. A. S. Adams in his *Enscotidion; or, Shadow of Death* described their logic as follows:

> Hell is a hole, where men are cooked by steam,
>   Is many a preacher's sermon boiled to jelly.
> Heaven is an ice-house, where the richest cream
>   Will soothe the appetite and cool the belly.
> And heaven's as heavenly as you ever saw;
>   And you had better go to heaven, I tell ye,
> Or hell will get you, bones and all, blood raw,
> And on them, when they're cooked, the Devil fill
>   his maw.[13]

One Methodist preacher, recalled W. H. Venable, was so enthusiastic about the heaven he was recommending to his Kentucky congregation and so eager for them to know its beauty, that he concluded his description thus: "In short, my brethren, to say all in one word, heaven is a Kentuck of a place!" [14] The terrifying loudness of the "firebrand's" voice, his fierce looks and vehement gesticulations made the sinful more and more conscious of their fallen state and their need to be born again. His appeal to sentiment, too, activated their consciences. Such an appeal was the following, by John A. Broadus:

> If you ever live to stand by your father's or your mother's grave, or stand, as I have stood, where both sleep side by side, and remember any time when you gave them pain by disobedience, oh then you will mourn most bitterly! It will be too late then, however you might desire it, to ask their pardon. Do not run the risk of ever knowing an hour of such keen agony—such bitter sorrow.[15]

Often early preachers held the attention of their audiences with their numerous antics and ingenious techniques. Some were almost as sensational as the famed Billy Sunday of somewhat modern times, who smashed chairs, leaped over tables, and stood on his head to clinch a point or create a mood in his appeal to the average American's love for excitement. The preacher Thompson, for example, would dance and mumble praises of God. James Russell would leap from the pulpit crying, "All who want religion, follow me." And out into the woods he would run with his congregation following in hot pursuit. There he would finish his discourse by calling for the "mourners" to come forward. Some speakers might even march around the church several times exhorting and singing hymns. William McGee would sometimes stand among the throng, sit, or lie in the dust, exhorting, "his eyes streaming, and his heart so full that he could only ejaculate, 'Jesus, Jesus!'"

Uncultivated itinerants, surprisingly, added greatly to

the South's reputation for producing men of eloquence. They traveled from month to month through beautiful forests and over picturesque hills, with considerable time and range for meditation, if not for systematic reading. The complexity of nature taught them something of God's handiwork. Their loneliness and need for companionship made them, like the prophets of old, men who "walked and talked" with God. Henry Fowler has described quite aptly the art of these discourses:

> The sermon has been built up day after day, by reflection on horseback, study in cabins, and practice through its growth, three or four times a week. All the varied experiences with nature, with people, in conversation, by anecdote, on the road, in the cabin, through the field, are made to contribute to its life; and thus, when finished, it is like its robust originator, hearty and elastic, full of vitality and blood and electricity, instead of being pale and abstract, like the dyspeptic clinger to rocking-chairs and book-encircled rooms.[16]

Men who traveled on horseback naturally acquired a pensive and a romantic turn of thought and expression, conducive to eloquence. Consequently, their preaching came to be of a highly popular cast. The primary appeal was to the feelings. No wonder, then, that, after long periods of living apart from mankind, musing in wood and on prairie, these men stirred up excitement and set off "awakenings." Timothy Flint is almost poetic as he writes of such an itinerant:

> A man of rude, boisterous, but native eloquence rises among these children of the forest and simple nature, with his voice pitched upon the tones, and his utterance filled with that awful theme, to which every string of the human heart every where responds; and while the woods echo his vehement declamations, his audience is alternately dissolved in tears, awed to profound feeling, or falling in spasms.[17]

He observes further that this country opens a boundless theater for strong, earnest, and unlettered eloquence like that of the circuit preacher.

His mind was richly endowed with the fruits of varied experiences, with an understanding of common things and common people, and above all, with a strong conviction. Too, his sincerity, simplicity, and faith in the importance of his task even in private conversation made him speak convincingly. David Crockett in his *Autobiography* writes glowingly of such a man's eloquence. As the two rode through the forest together, he says, they talked about politics, religion, nature, farming, bear-hunting, and an all-bountiful Providence. When they began to develop the latter topic, the old minister's

> imagination glowed, and his soul became full to overflowing; and he checked his horse, and I stopped mine also, and a stream of eloquence burst forth from his aged lips, such as I have seldom listened to: it came from the overflowing fountain of a pure and grateful heart. We were alone in the wilderness, but as he proceeded it seemed to me as if the tall trees bent their tops to listen; that the mountain stream laughed out joyfully as it bounded on like some living thing, that the fading flowers of autumn smiled, and sent forth fresher fragrance, as if conscious that they would revive in spring; and even the sterile rocks seemed to be endued with some mysterious influence. We were alone in the wilderness, but all things told me that God was there.[18]

So powerful and effective were the old man's words that Crockett no longer felt weak and alone in a strange land. He believed now with his riding companion that whether one lived in the populous city or alone in a pathless forest, whether one was of low or high degree, the ever-watchful Eye was there. Crockett's eyes were wet with tears as he rode closer to his companion to press his arm and thank him.

The fruits of the harvest further bespeak the eloquence and accomplishments of the itinerant preacher. Poets, novelists, and biographers have been extravagant in their praise. The poetess Amelia Coppuck Welby, for example, captures something of the depth of pulpit eloquence when she writes:

> Such language as his I may never recall;
> But his theme was salvation—salvation to all;
> And the souls of a thousand in ecstasy hung
> On the manna-like sweetness that dropped
>   from his tongue;
> Not alone on the ear his wild eloquence stole;
> Enforced by each gesture it sank to the soul,
> Till it seemed that an angel had brightened the sod
> And brought to each bosom a message from God.[19]

The speaker's description of Christ's suffering and of the cross gave his sermon a dramatic effect. "The gush of bright crimson that flowed from his side" was effectively depicted. The man's "charm in delivery," the expression in his eyes, and the movement of his lips made manifest the sincerity of his appeal. Amelia recalls, too, how much she was impressed by his concluding gestures, his whispering of Jesus and pointing above.

William Gilmore Simms, occasionally inserting religious elements in his novels, turns in *Guy Rivers, A Tale of Georgia* to characterize the itinerant. His minister, however, is not the thundering type: "His matter and manner, alike, are distinguished by modest good sense, a gentle and dignified ease and spirit, and a pleasing earnestness in his object that is never offensive." [20] Although mild and gentle, he was dramatic. After the hymn, he read in a clear and unaffected voice the Twenty-third Psalm—a passage of Scripture that blended with the rustic setting in the wilderness. Not offering any one of the verses as a text and not explaining doubtful passages of little meaning, like so many "small teachers" of his day, he simply elaborated upon "those beautiful portraits of a good shepherd and guardian God." The dependence of man with which he introduced the countenance of Providence; the dangers of the forest, with which he introduced the mysteries of life—these he expounded at great length. The destruction of fields and cattle, the blighting of crops, and the demolition of homes were among the numberless events he discussed. Then, after showing how helpless man is under such circumstances, he pointed out the willingness of the Creator to assume a protectorate over him. God, he says, would shield him. Then he adds:

> It was poetry, indeed—sweet poetry—but it was the poetry of truth and not of fiction. Did not history sustain its every particular? Had not the Shepherd made them to lie down in green pastures—had he not led them beside the still waters—restored he not their souls—did he not lead them, for his name's sake, in the paths of righteousness—and though at length they walked through the valley where Death had cast his never departing shadow, was he not with them still, keeping them even from the fear of the evil? He furnished them with the rod and staff; he prepared the repast for them, even in the presence of their enemies; he anointed their heads with oil, and blessed them with quiet and abundance, until they even ceased to doubt that goodness and mercy should follow them all the days of their life; and, with a proper consciousness of the source whence this great flood has arisen, they determined, with the spirit not less of wise than of worthy men, to follow his guidance, and thus dwell in the house of the Lord for ever.[21]

As he assured the audience of this same divine protection that was given to the patriarchs, his declamation became bold and beautiful. Not a whisper or a sound was perceptible in the assembly—all eyes were focused on the forest preacher. He was eloquent in the true sense!

William Wirt, author of *The Letters of the British*

Spy, is glowing in his appraisal of a sermon he heard in an out-of-the-way place in Virginia. James Waddell, the blind preacher, spoke on a subject Wirt had heard developed a thousand times, but he breathed new life into his topic. "As he descended from the pulpit to distribute the mystic symbols, there was a peculiar, a more than human solemnity in his air and manner, which," says Wirt, "made my blood run cold, and my whole frame shiver." The sufferings of Christ, the trial before Pilate, the ascent up Calvary, the crucifixion and death were narrated in such a way that the material became a new story. His enunciation was deliberate, his voice quivering on every syllable, the audience even trembling in unison as he dramatized his subject. So vivid was his presentation that the congregation at one point actually became indignant with the Jews. When he approached the climax of his sermon—Christ on the cross—his voice became fainter and fainter, until, for the force of his own feelings, he could not speak; then he raised his handkerchief to his eyes and burst into a flood of tears. The congregation groaned, shrieked, and sobbed. When the tumult finally subsided, he revealed his dramatic power even more as he quoted one short line from Rousseau: "Socrates died like a philosopher, but Jesus Christ, like a God!" As he whispered the last part he clasped his hands and looked to heaven.[22]

The speaker's peculiar type of eloquence, his understanding of the yeoman mind, his adaptability, sincerity, unselfishness, and asceticism contributed largely to his success. As William Gilmore Simms writes in his novel *Charlemont,* he was generally not one of those sorry, self-constituted representatives of man's eternal interests who deluge their audiences with vain and worthless declamations, "proving that virtue is a very good thing, religion a very commendable virtue, and a liberal contribution to the church-box at the close of the sermon one of the most decided proofs that we have this virtue in perfection." [23] His interests were not in material things, as his life manifested. Simms adds cogently:

> He was not one of those fine preachers who, dealing out counsels of self-denial, in grave saws and solemn maxims, with wondrous grim visage and a most slow, lugubrious shaking of the head—are yet always religiously careful to secure the warmest seat by the fire-side, and the best buttered bun on the table.[24]

He had no systematic or scientific training, his chief virtue being an aptness for popular discourse and exhortation. He seemed to speak without method, nor was his attention to either grammar or logic very rigid; yet he revealed a power, an unction about both matter and manner, that got within his listener immediately, often to set him weeping before he knew it. This type of preacher was best suited for breaking the ground in new regions. His ignorance became his blessing and treasure. Often, according to Cartwright, he even prided himself on having "never rubbed his back against the walls of a college," where he might have lost his knowledge of how to catch fish in the net of the Kingdom of God. Since the people in the early days along the frontiers were so uninformed, the preacher could bring together a few simple ideas in short order to supply all their spiritual needs; hence he had no use for a formal education. However, by the 1830's, people were beginning to expect more of the pulpit; consequently, both Methodists and Baptists a few years later made a modest start by establishing schools and seminaries to train their raw recruits. They even began providing increased support to journals and periodicals that gave some outlet for their intellectual zeal.

Actually in the early days of the itinerant system the minister had little time, inclination, or facilities for "letters." He frequently camped out in the mountains or

found a night's lodging in a log cabin. Such a life was
not conducive to serious study. His purpose was not so
much to develop the mind but to connect the scattered
settlements with a bond of friendly and moral interest.
Evaluating his accomplishments in his *Sketches of History, Life, and Manners,* James Hall wrote in 1835:

> Had it not been for the labours of these indefatigable
> men, our country, as to a great extent of its settlement,
> would have been at this day, a semi-barbarous region.
> How many thousands, and tens of thousands, of the most
> ignorant and licentious of our population, have they in-
> structed and reclaimed from the error of their ways?
> They have restored to society even the most worthless,
> and made them valuable and respectable as citizens, and
> useful in all the relations of life. Their numerous and
> zealous ministry bids fair to carry on the good work to
> any extent which our settlements and population may
> require.[25]

Day by day the itinerant went about his work of preaching, reforming the wayward, burying the dead, chris-
tening the young, marrying the lovers, establishing
churches, and participating often as master of ceremonies in rural festivities of a sane sort. He was more than
a physician for the lame of soul and spirit; he was often
an amateur medic who looked after the ills of the body
as well. Scarcely was the little cabin built and the
timber cleared for plowing before the evangelical
teacher was there to give the new land his blessing and
to collect the folk into societies. He opened a new
region, which was to him a realm that promised not so
much new lands and earthly riches as a kingdom serving God, whose public relations man he was par ex-
cellence.

When tired and worn out, itinerants—whether rough
and thunderous or gentle and sublime—experienced
the same end: retirement or superannuation. To save
enough money for a comfortable old age was impossi-

ble on their salaries. Some Methodists, if fortunate, were paid small stipends, but the money was actually not enough to buy a good suit of clothes and have much left over for necessities. But in those days homespun was in style. By way of comparison, Presbyterian ministers fared a little better, often being allotted $200 annually. Even so, their lot was likewise a hard one, their material rewards not ensuring economic security in their declining years.

Usually the retired preacher lived through the "setting sun" of his career in retrospect. He might be pictured poetically, in the terms of John C. Keener in *The Post-Oak Circuit*, as an old man leaning on his staff at the small cottage door, to whom a granddaughter brings an evening meal of milk and bread. Each evening she asks him the same questions, partly to delight him but mainly to hear him reminisce in stories identical each time in form and content:

> "For forty-five years I received an appointment as an itinerant preacher from our dear bishops. But from the waters of the Monongahela down to the Attakapas country the greater part of my life as a preacher was spent."

Then, as always, she would ask about his experience with the Indians, and he would reply:

> "Yes, indeed, Grandpa has many a time preached through an interpreter. Many a time have I slept in the woods; for years, as often there as elsewhere. This whole country was then thinly settled. I labored hereabouts, and all over the West and South-west, among the early settlers."

She would ask him if it was not a hard life, and again he revealed his usual optimism:

> "It was a very glorious life, my dearest; yes, a hard life, but a useful, noble toil. O, would that I could still preach

the gospel to poor sinners, and minister consolation to the people of God!"

Seeing his threadbare coat, she would ask, "Were you poor then, Grandpa?" to which he would reply without shame, "Yes, my dear, I was poor then too—often very poor; though sometimes I had a little beforehand." [26] Through revival meetings and peripatetic evangelism, within the framework of gospel Christianity, the traveling preacher laid the cornerstone of the South's religious structure. For more than one hundred years he braved the elements to plant a culture in the wilderness. His dogged persistence, most notably in the case of the Methodists, immortalized the circuit-rider system, which required numerous visitations in log cabins, at least one Bible class per week, and as many as three sermons daily. The old farmer was correct when he remarked one cold, rainy morning as he looked through the windowpane, "There is nothing out today but crows and Methodist preachers." Rain or shine, he kept his appointments, sometimes, as in the case of Lorenzo Dow, made as much as a year in advance. From the time of Bishop Francis Asbury on into the latter half of the nineteenth century the traveling minister followed the advancing frontier and rode from log cabin to log meetinghouse, or from church to church, and back again, touching as many as forty points along the way. Methodists used the circuit system most effectively, but Baptists, Disciples, and sometimes Presbyterians employed an itinerant clergy also. It was necessity's own creation in frontier America, where society was mobile.

The itinerant was most active during the first half of the nineteenth century, but his reason for being continued until the last frontier had been reached and populated. The Civil War might be regarded as the climax of his long life, for thereafter we see only the waning years of his toilsome existence.[27]

Several factors contributed to the itinerant's departure from the Southern scene. The process of urbanization led to the settled preacher. The greater emphasis upon education and theological training drove many unlettered men out of the profession. Finally, improved transportation facilities—better roads and vehicles—enabled more and more people to attend the larger meetings in town or community center. But in sparsely settled areas of America the need for his service continued into the twentieth century, for he carried spiritual sustenance to an isolated people who were too few to establish more than scattered fellowships and small churches.

Functioning simultaneously were the so-called "city preachers" and theologians, men like Thomas Smyth and James Henley Thornwell, both distinguished Presbyterians. The settled preachers were responsible for most of the literary output during the period, since they had the inclination and the leisure for writing. Although many of them did not venture far beyond their seminaries or pulpits, they managed to keep abreast of the times. They took the raw material of frontier Christianity and adapted it in more finished form to a changing society. They also indulged in the doctrinal controversies which characterized the era. Perhaps the established ministers preserved what the academician would call formalism, but the bulk of them—in particular the Methodists and Baptists—carried on actively the movement of evangelism that had begun in the camp meetings.

In the transition from the traveling preacher to the settled clergyman several familiar institutions passed away, e.g., the one-room log schoolhouse as the center of religious culture, and the old farmhouse, which opened its doors to the man who taught the "right doctrine." Less popular also became the service in the forest with a ceiling of giant oak trees and a floor of green and scattered leaves. An old-timer upon reading Simms's novel *Guy Rivers* will have feelings of nostalgia as the author re-creates the atmosphere of a service in the out-of-doors:

> A few fallen trees, trimmed of their branches and touched with the adze, ranging at convenient distances under the boughs of those along with which they had lately stood up in proud equality, furnished seats for the now rapidly-gathering assemblage. A rough stage, composed of logs, rudely hewn and crossing each other at right angles, covered when at a height of sufficient elevation, formed the pulpit from which the preacher was to exhort. A chair, brought from some cottage in the neighborhood, surmounted the stage. This was all that art had done to accommodate nature to the purposes of man.
>
> In the body of the wood immediately adjacent, fastened to overhanging branches, were the goodly steeds of the company. . . . Some, more docile than the rest, were permitted to rove at large, cropping the young herbage and tender grass; occasionally, . . . during the service, overleaping their limits in a literal sense; neighing, whinnying and kicking up their heels to the manifest confusion of the pious and the discomfiture of the preacher.[28]

In such an atmosphere Southern Christianity had its beginning. Methodism, particularly, liked the open air with just the simple kind of furniture that nature provided. The first churches were the log cabins, where a chair in the open doorway served as a pulpit; beds, rough boards, and a loft as seats. Paul Neff Garber reminisces in *The Methodist Meeting House* about the general surroundings: "The tethered horses, the waving grain without, the deep silence of nature, undisturbed save by the song of the rustic worshipers or the voice of the preacher, blended into a scene which no one who has been a participant in such a scene can ever forget." [29] Even barns served the pioneer itinerant when the homes were too small to accommodate the crowds. Sometimes they moved under brush arbors, and very often to community schoolhouses, where all denominations might attempt to participate—not always, though, without dispute over doctrine. Courthouses, taverns, even boats were among the meeting-houses in the early days.

With the passing of the rural preacher and his taste for simplicity in places of worship came a new type of sanctuary—a small, neat, Grecian temple, glimmering white and saint-like through the groves.[30] Perhaps it was a building of discolored stone, with a large elm waving its boughs above, shading the final resting-place of its more prominent members. The windows and doors were surmounted by little roofs, supported by iron rods. A stone slab lay before each entrance. The floor was of flagstone, the pews high with their Puritan-straight backs. On the walls of the chancel, wrote John Esten Cooke in his novel *The Virginia Comedians,* were inscribed the rigid code of the congregation—the laws of Moses.[31]

And as the itinerant was supplanted by the settled preacher and the forest pulpit succeeded by the tiny church in the township, so also the smaller edifices yielded to larger and more modern ones. George W. Bagby, Virginia author and editor, writes poetically of this transition. Near the City Hotel of Lynchburg, he says, stands a sacred furniture warehouse: the empty belfry perched upon the gable tells the stranger that only a nameless spirit now lingers around its form. The old-fashioned plain benches and the deep-toned bell are gone.

Here religion, in its terror and its tenderness, in the sublimity of its hopes and the boundlessness of its despair, was preached by lips fired almost to prophecy; here prayers as pure as ever trembled up to God's throne were uttered; and here repentance as sincere as ever transformed erring men was felt and avowed.[32]

But new times demanded new churches. The sacred edifice at Lynchburg gave way to one whose "Gothic beauty deserves the admiration it has received." Its organ, touched by the master's hand, uttered a glorious voice, but this finer architecture and more melodious music could not make one forget that humble structure, the simple manners, and the plain hymn music and singers of earlier times—the days when the traveling preacher was in his prime.

5

The Spirit
of Sectarianism

THE FIRST THREE DECADES of the nineteenth century were marked by a series of emotional upheavals fomented by the "Great Revival." During this period the camp meeting became an institution in frontier America, and the gospel missionary, a legend. The Negro slave became an indispensable commodity both in the labor market and for the purposes of establishing representation. Counting as three fifths of one person in the census, he gave the Old South added strength in the national political scene, until the extension of slavery was restricted.

A section that had been marked by indifference and paganism was now moving toward a type of religious solidarity. Salvation had become a topic of conversation in the South.

The period from 1830 to the Civil War was one of sectionalism in both religion and politics. Division and subdivision of churches were common, with each sect affirming its loyalty to certain doctrines, forms of worship, and practices. Loyalty to denomination had precedence over fidelity to a common ethical philosophy. Historian William Warren Sweet observes that the era was characterized by quarrels, contentions, and slanders among religionists.[1] Actually the entire first half of the nineteenth century gave the appearance of restlessness, for controversies had begun taking shape when the first spiritual fire was ignited on the frontier. Jesse Laney Boyd writes that preaching became largely controversial, and that religious debates were "popular, also sometimes characterized by rancorous bitterness, when excitement ran high as a champion of the Baptists measured lances with a leading controversialist of another denomination." [2]

Contemporary observers concur in their evaluation of the religious mind during the first half of the century. It was truly a period of storm and stress. William Faux affirmed that the bitter sectarian spirit was even more vicious than it was in England, probably being stimulated by a miserable, petty feeling of aristocracy. Although religion became the theme on Sunday, the presence of intolerance made the worshiper forget that this was a day of worship. Faux says:

> Methodists predominate and are brimful of bigotry; and the Catholics are very fiery and violent in all spiritual matters, but, having no power, they cannot injure their fellow-citizens. All sects hate my reverend friend because he is an Unitarian, and hates slavery, and therefore nothing good can be in him or come out of him.[3]

Opposition might even be expressed in violence, as it was McGready's experience in Kentucky about twenty years earlier, when his vehement preaching stirred up so much objection from the formalists that they burned his pulpit and pews.[4]

Not only method but matter, too, provoked disputation. A great deal of the early preaching was doctrinal, often metaphysical, and most religious conversation was similar in kind. Some of the topics were revival meetings, election, reprobation, predestination, infant baptism, sprinkling, immersion, and closed communion. There was so much difference of opinion that ministers appeared to be in constant warfare; and society itself, says Thomas Hamilton, was torn into shreds and patches, varying in color, form, and texture.[5]

The results of such a condition were several. Rural areas and small townships particularly were hardest hit by the impact of dissension. A community that was scarcely able to fill one church found itself divided, and even smaller groups indulged in argument, dispute, and bitterness of feeling within their own ranks. For example, a Socinian would not object to hearing an Arian minister, but he refused to listen to a Trinitarian; the Calvinist would consent sometimes to an exponent of "free agency," if he accepted certain absolute decrees; the Baptist would surrender a favorite dogma, but he would never tolerate a speaker who did not stress adult baptism as an absolute essential.[6] Under such conditions, doctrinal warfare seemed inevitable. Apparent victory for a particular sect did not settle disputes and make for harmony; instead, there was only a deepening of jealousies, antipathies, and rivalry among communicants and preachers. Rival clergymen attacked each other in the pulpit and through the press so frequently that they became increasingly bigoted and dogmatic. For example, Charles Murray indicates something of the argumentative and confident tone reflected in a Presbyterian sermon at Frankfort, Kentucky:

> I heard a curious sermon, contending from the analogy of nature to numerous texts in Scripture, that there is but one way in which man can be saved, and but one right and saving faith among the various sects of Christianity. The argument was sometimes well supported; but the discourse appeared to me to fall into an error very common to such subjects, namely, to prove too much.[7]

A Baptist minister by the name of David Thurman had become so afflicted by the argumentative tradition that one day he openly lamented to his congregation his lack of success and sought their advice. The aged widow of John LaRue promptly interrupted his sermon and pointed her finger in his face, saying, "I'll tell you what is the matter, Brother Thurman, stop preaching John Calvin and James Arminius, and preach Jesus Christ." J. H. Spencer records that Thurman took her advice and delivered a successful revivalistic sermon on the text "I determined not to know any thing among you, save Jesus Christ, and him crucified." [8]

Visitors to the South made generalizations about the religious culture which they found. They pointed out that Southern Christianity lacked a beauty of worship,[9] a genuine mysticism, an appreciation of the historical church, and a cultural tradition. Exclusive of Presbyterian and Episcopalian clergy, the ministry was accused of not possessing a profound and spiritual theology. Attacks by Methodists upon abstract intellectualism and rationalism in the Presbyterian churches and decadence in the Episcopal churches had a tendency to shift the emphasis from theology per se to creeds and moralism. The frontier spirit so shaped the emotional structure of religion that old-world formalism in worship, including the techniques at the sacramental table, the use of cross, baptismal font, and gown, gave way to preaching, free prayer, and vehement singing.[10] Such a shift in interest was due primarily to the efforts of Methodists (Arminians) and Baptists, who, in seeking out the great mass, encountered a segment of the population that was culturally, economically, and socially among the lower group. Where economic security did not exist, the desire for the soul's security in the life hereafter came to be of even greater concern. Sometimes a whole area became infected with an inspired urgency for salvation.[11]

Another source of intolerance grew out of the free use of a democratic privilege. The shift away from established churches gave rise to sectarianism (called denominationalism when the special group lost its original effectiveness, enthusiasm, or prestige). The

freedom of worship allowed in a democracy only has-
tened and encouraged sectarian feuds, even provoking
disunity, controversy, and confusion within a particular
group itself. In his series of lectures on American life,
Philip Schaff deplored its many evils, such as the use of
unfair methods of furthering particular ends; the nurtur-
ing of party spirit and passion, envy, selfishness, and
bigotry; the transformation of a peaceful kingdom into a
battlefield where brother fights brother, neighbor attacks neighbor; the sacrifice of church universal for
party; and, most important of all, the abuse of Christ by
casting him in the firebrand of jealousy.[12]

The Old South, with the frontier heritage of an absence of restraint, became a congenial climate for a
reformed type of religion. American traditions of freedom and equality protected the numerous Protestant
sects. They are all in the Southern sector, and, says
Schaff, "not rarely half a dozen in a single country
town, each with its own church or chapel; and, where
they have any real vitality at all, they grow there pro-
portionally much faster than in Europe." [13]

The three most important Southern sects were the
Baptist, Methodist, and Presbyterian—in the order of
their size. With conflicts between the Northern and
Southern branches over political issues came the development of a sectional bias and finally separation. "Each
of these denominations was started solely to serve the
South," writes E. DeForest Leach, "for the reason that
the South was considered socially and religiously in-
compatible with the rest of the country." [14]

A fourth sect was the Disciples of Christ, which sponsored an indigenous, reformed culture. Though his
sect was the product of a reaction against creedalism,
which was regarded as the source of sectarian warfare,
Alexander Campbell was swept into the stream of doctrinal controversy. Influential as a group appealing for
simplicity, in the upper sections—Kentucky, Tennessee, and adjacent areas—the Disciples moved ahead of

the Presbyterians. There were many other religious groups, but only those already mentioned played a dominant role in the Old South in preparing the climate for a type of orthodoxy identified with the Bible Belt. One might puncture any sectarian skin and the same orthodox blood would flow.

These four rival denominations debated the propriety of religious controversy. Many churchmen decried disputation in order to destroy free inquiry; some despised it because they did not like to be contradicted; others spoke against it to be spared the embarrassment of showing their own ignorance or to be saved the effort of defending their own views; and still others avoided controversy because of the evil temper with which the debates were too frequently conducted.

Although there were some Southerners who objected to free inquiry for the reasons above, there were many ministers who gave public approval to it as a means of getting at the fundamentals in religion. Thomas Smyth, a prominent Presbyterian minister, sets forth what some leaders proclaimed: In the spirit of the "true warfaring Christians" of Milton's *Areopagitica,* "not only ministers . . . but *every Christian* is a warrior, under the Captain of his own salvation, and under obligation to contend earnestly for the faith, and not to sell it." With the dust and heat of battle would come final victory:

> They must hold it [faith] fast, by persevering devotion to it, and by a zealous defence of it, lest "being led away by the error of the wicked, they fall from their steadfastness, and at last lose their crown." For he that is content to be a looker-on, while his fellow Christians contend earnestly for the faith, shall never be more than a looker-on when they are crowned with that diadem which is laid up for them who have "kept the faith." [15]

It was pointed out that the Prince of Peace never sheathed the sword of the spirit while he lived: "He drew it on the banks of the Jordan and threw the scabbard away." [16] Many preachers justified their own aggressiveness further by citing Christ's driving the money changers from the temple and his courage before Pilate and the rabid mob. They reasoned that Christ foresaw the necessity for conflict, that the true Christian, while he carries the olive branch in one hand, must keep in the other a strong sword to beat down those who would suppress the true gospel.

The efficacy of free inquiry came to be recognized. James King, in the first issue of the *Calvinistic Magazine* (1846), points out that we should throw ourselves open to the arguments of our brother who proposes to examine our creed and test our ideas by the word of truth: "I for one do not want to be let alone. If I am building wood, hay and stubble, he is my friend who informs me of it. If my house is on the sand, for heaven's sake let me know it before the rain descends and the winds beat." [17] Free discussion and controversy on the street, in the parlor, or in the pulpit some believed would help to eliminate ignorance, bigotry, and error.[18] This interplay of ideas, they maintained, would give new vigor to the mind, would enlighten men upon all subjects, in all the arts and sciences, in all things philosophical, literary, moral, and political. Alexander Campbell voiced his view in regard to controversy, showing its effects upon research and human progress thus:

> It was the tongue and pen of controversy which developed the true solar system—laid the foundation for the American Revolution—abolished the slave trade—and which has so far disenthralled the human mind from the shackles of superstition. Locke and Sidney, Milton and Newton, were all controversialists and reformers, philosophers literary—religious and political. . . . [If there had been no disputation,] neither the Jewish nor the Christian religion could have ever been established; nor had it

ceased could the Reformation have ever been achieved. It has been the parent of almost all the social blessings which we enjoy.[19]

Needless to say, it was not this positive and constructive type of disputation, but the negative type that helped give the South its later peculiar, belligerent conservatism and the atmosphere we have observed. There was a type of disputation that all Southern ministers feared, that in which the conflict sprang from a mere spirit of contention, from the desire for victory, the love of display, or from personal animosity rather than from the love of truth.[20] If the conflict dealt with unimportant issues, if it became the vehicle of personal malignity and was conducted in a spirit that severed the bonds of charity and peace, it was labeled unchristian.[21]

The churches originally approved free inquiry and discussion, but when denominations became more competitive, they began to abuse the freedom which existed in the American system of denominationalism. They engaged in two types of dispute—guerrilla warfare (or internal dissension) and sectarian warfare along a broad battlefront.

Before the Civil War, churches became particularly plagued by strife within their own ranks. They were torn by the economic and political implications of slavery, by the theological problems surrounding predestination, missions, and an educated ministry—to mention only a few of the problems. While the denominations were wrestling with forces within their midst, they were contesting with rival sects on issues that seem insignificant today but that reached major proportions by the time of secession. Some of these issues were revivalism, preacher-training, the existence of Catholic elements in ritual and doctrine, predestination, election, the methods of baptism, infant baptism, open versus closed communion—to cite those most bitterly contested.

The effect of these issues upon the major denominations is material for more exhaustive treatment than here proposed and is certainly too entangled and stultifying for more than a surface consideration. However, the subject of revivalism and the camp meeting is of such general interest that it requires more than a passing reference.

As already indicated, the mammoth outdoor services may have been instrumental in calming many a sinful heart, particularly among those on the lower levels of society, and may have accelerated interest in religion. Yet they provoked an unfavorable reaction among most Presbyterians and Episcopalians. On the one hand, revival meetings united a horde of sinners in their quest of the "New Jerusalem." On the other hand, they accentuated certain social, doctrinal, and theological differences that had previously been inconsequential in an agrarian section.

Numerous objections were raised. Chief among them were complaints that the meetings encouraged disorderly behavior in public worship, that they made for immorality and too free communication of the sexes, promulgated doctrinal errors, and provoked spurious conversions by emphasis upon a strictly emotional appeal rather than a rational one.

L. A. Lowry presents the Presbyterian objection to the "Big Meeting" in a letter to his father, as he points out the injurious effect on the cause of religion and morality:

I allude to the disgraceful scenes so often witnessed in Arminian churches, which some are pleased to call revivals of religion—where the sympathies and passions are worked upon by every possible means, and combined and concerted effort put forth to make people religious by the instrumentality of mourners' benches, anxious seats, shouting committees, ranting exhortations, and such like—where noise and devotion are considered synonymous, and the effect of the whole scene depen-

dent upon the confusion that results from the extra-or-
dinary means employed.[22]

Because of the confused and disorderly audience, even
those who were sympathetic toward revivalism wondered about the values involved. Naturally those who
had come to find fault saw little to praise—what with
people fainting, friends rushing to their aid, several sermons or hymns in progress simultaneously throughout
the expansive grounds, and the violent behavior among
those affected.

Perhaps the most serious objection to the outdoor
meetings was the belief that they fostered immorality.
The vast crowds which assembled in the woods included many irreligious people, for not everyone came
in search of salvation. Among this motley crew were the
blackleg, the cutpurse, the prostitute, and the flotsam
and jetsam of frontier days. Hucksters sold raw whiskey
from their wagons on the outskirts of the campgrounds,
and gamblers and horse traders were busy exploiting
the gullible.

Perhaps the most serious problem was the too-free
communication of the sexes, which led to strict rules
being set up and incorporated into the camp-meeting
manuals for the controlling of activities at night. The
sexes were separated during the hours allotted to sleep,
with night watchmen constantly policing the grounds.
Even in the daytime a sharp discipline was necessary,
for, as Robert Davidson quotes from Lyle's Diary,
"women, in their frantic agitations, often unconsciously
exposed their persons in a manner shocking to common
decency. Not only did they tear open their bosoms, but
they had sometimes to be held by main strength to
keep them from the most indelicate attitude." [23] Fe-
males under the spell of conviction sometimes hugged
and embraced everyone in their vicinity, and Davidson
charged that ministers were often at hand to receive a

liberal share of the embracing. In *Domestic Manners of the Americans,* Frances Trollope said that she was horrified at seeing the prostrate young girls receive from time to time mystic caresses from ministers. "More than once," she writes, "I saw a young neck encircled by a reverend arm. Violent hysterics and convulsions seized many of them, and when the tumult was at the highest, the preacher who remained above [on the platform], again gave out a hymn as if to drown it." [24] Presbyterians would note in a sarcastic vein that this ritual was no doubt intended as an imitation of the kiss of charity referred to in II Cor. 13:12, and I Thess. 5:26.

Excesses were numerous. The number of illegitimate births increased in proportion to the popularity of camp meetings. Some critics were so bold as to state that there were probably more souls created than saved at these barbaric outdoor festivals. Instances of misconduct and looseness of morals were quite common, according to contemporary observers. For example, one such observer reported: "Becca Bell,—who often fell, is now big with child to a wicked trifling school master of the name of Brown who says he'll be damned to hell if he ever marries her." "Raglin's daughter seems careless. . . . Kitty Cummings got careless. . . . Polly Moffitt was with child to Petty and died miserably in child bed." [25]

On one occasion, watchmen with burning pine knots stuck in their hats found six men under one altar with a strumpet.[26] In telling about the many orgies in the forest, John Lambert records: "They sleep together in tents, old and young; men, women, and children indiscriminately; the vigorous male near the unblushing female; black and white, all together." [27] Such a testimonial as this would naturally not improve relations between revivalists and their opponents, because it appeared to Methodists, for example, as a character assassination that could be refuted by reference to the regulations of the camp-meeting manual.

The unprecedented behavior of individuals who became involved in the religious "exercises," such as those loosely described as the "jumps," "barks," "falling," "running," "jerks," and "rolling," reveals that people under conviction often acted strangely and irrationally. The pulpit was frequently accused of inciting insincere emotions and casting hypnotic spells upon the unsuspecting; hence the charge was made that religion under these conditions was of a "mushroom" quality. With the ministers working to stir human passions—anxious to make a noise and raise a ferment—frequently some rather coarse human particles became entangled in the "gospel net." There was some justification for the criticism that many hopeful souls even came to take the vows of the church and to be baptized without understanding anything at all about what they were doing. The principal cause was believed to be an overemphasis on sudden conversions; in fact, Presbyterians charged that a sinner who "fell" one night from a sense of guilt or from emotional disturbance might "fall" the next from drinking too much raw whiskey.

To be sure, "the kiss of charity" and the excited female have been exploited by some who wear the cloth. Certainly there are accounts of immoralities during religious orgies, even in the twentieth century. Novelists like Sinclair Lewis, Erskine Caldwell, and John Steinbeck did not rely primarily on the imagination. Lewis was familiar with the Elmer Gantry type in the American pulpit. Steinbeck's Reverend Jim Casy in *The Grapes of Wrath* was the crown prince of the rogues. For example, the confession to Tom Joad reveals Casy's technique:

"I use to get the people jumpin' and talkin' in tongues, and glory-shoutin' till they just fell down an' passed out. An' some I'd baptize to bring 'em to. An' then you know what I'do?—I'd take one of them girls out in the grass,

an' I'd lay with her. Done it ever' time. Then I'd feel
bad, an' I'd pray and pray, but it didn't do no good.
Come the nex' time, them an' me was full of the spirit,
I'd do it again. I figgered there just wasn't no hope for
me, an' I was a damned ol' hypocrite. But I didn't mean
to be." [28]

But Casy was unwilling to assume all the blame, for he
thought the people lacked a sense of direction and a
concern:

"Here's me preachin' grace. An' here's them people get-
tin' grace so hard the're jumpin' and shoutin'. Now they
say layin' up with a girl comes from the devil. But the
more grace a girl got in her, the quicker she wants to go
out in the grass. An' I got to thinkin' how in hell s'cuse
me, how can the devil get in when a girl is so full of the
Holy Spirit that it's spoutin' out of her nose an' ears.
You'd think that that'd be one time when the devil didn't
stand a snowball's chance in hell. But there it was." [29]

No doubt the controversies growing out of revivalism
were among the most heated that developed during the
early period in the South, but by the 1850's the opponents were becoming accustomed to upheavals and
recognized that the good overshadowed the ill effects.

Other types of disputation followed the conflict over
revivalism. The Old South was the scene of many sectarian battles over predestination, baptism, and closed
communion, both sides being vehemently and pe-
dantically presented. In the earlier part of the nineteenth century the Arminians (Methodists) and Calvinists (Presbyterians) occupied the center of the stage,
but pedobaptists and Baptists were equally capable of
attracting attention. Debates were common, but acri-
monious pamphlets and tracts, including pseudo-lit-
erary doctrinal novels, were numerous. The sermons
particularly reflected the spirit of the times, with their
argumentative tone.

Another topic of controversy was the education of

ministers. The demand for raising standards in the pulpit stirred up considerable strife among frontier peoples. The most ignorant were the first to resist change. Baptist farmer preachers took pride in their ignorance and lack of training, recalling pleasantly the fact that Jesus' twelve disciples had been simple and unlearned men. "What good would an education do me," said one Baptist preacher, "as long as I've got plenty of wind?" B. F. Riley in *A History of the Baptists in States East of the Mississippi* reflects a typical objection to a formal education of preachers:

> We view theological schools [as] unwarranted in the word of God and dangerous to religious liberty. And wherever they have been organized, whether Jewish, Pagan, Heathen, Roman Catholic, they have been a source of persecution and bloodshed on the church of Christ.[30]

Peter Cartwright speaks for the Methodists in his objection to a trained ministry for frontier and sparsely settled areas: "I have seen so many of these educated preachers who forcibly remind me of lettuce growing under the shade of a peach-tree, or like a gosling that had got the straddles by wading in the dew, that I turned away sick and faint." [31]

Among the Baptists, opposition to education, missions, and Bible and tract societies was strongest between 1820 and 1840. According to Hosea Holcombe in *A History of the Rise and Progress of the Baptists in Alabama,* a plain, old man who was a licensed Baptist preacher was called upon to explain what it was he had against missionaries. After considerable "humming and hawing" he divulged both a bias and a fear:

> "I don't know nothing about them missionaries that go off to the heathen yonder, they tell us about, but what must they come amongst us for? If we allow them to come into our churches, the people will all go to hear

them preach, and won't go to hear us preach, and WE SHALL ALL BE PUT DOWN." [32]

The bitterness of the controversy is contained in another testimony reported by Riley:

> "Do not forget the enemy [the missionaries]; bear them in mind; the howling destructive wolves, the ravenous dogs, and the filthy and their numerous whelps. By a minute observation and the consultation of the sacred, never-failing, descriptive chart, even their physiognomy in dress, mien, and carriage, and many other indented, indelible, descriptive marks, too tedious at present to write. The wolfish smell is enough to alarm, to create suspicion, and to ascertain; the dogs' teeth are noted, and the wolves for their peculiar and distinctive howl, etc." [33]

Spencer, in sampling Baptist feeling in Kentucky, reports an incident in which a layman by the name of McMurry was called before his governing board to answer for the contribution of one dollar to missions. Just before his case went to the jury, he made a tactical move that prevented his exclusion from the Baptist Church. McMurry handed his keys to one of the leaders in his church, saying: "Here is the key to my corn crib, this one will admit you into my meat house, and the third one unlocks my money drawer. Take them and dispose of my possessions as you think most to the glory of God." [34]

Sharp disagreements and dissension arose over societies established to enlighten frontier peoples. The American Tract Society and American Bible Society were supported by the Presbyterian Church, but their usefulness was questioned by some Baptist and Methodist leaders. The Methodist James B. Finley feared that the religious books would divert the mind from the Bible and that the many benevolent associations would also divert the mind from the church.

Walter Posey, in his lectures entitled *Religious Strife on the Southern Frontier*, reports the prejudice of "Parson" William G. Brownlow, Methodist preacher, politician, and newspaper editor from eastern Tennessee. Brownlow, with a deep antipathy for Calvinists, attacked the Presbyterians for dominating the board of directors of the American Tract Society. He accused the American Home Missionary Society of sending "little college-bred chaps and theological scavengers" through the West "prowling and skulking about our country, from one rich neighborhood to another, making proselytes and begging money." His attack on the American Bible Society, which was regulated by Presbyterians and Congregationalists, was the most vicious. He pointed out that there appeared to be a misappropriation of funds when each free Bible represented a cost of $8.91, a figure that he contrasted with the low production costs of the Methodist Book Concern.[35]

Controversy over associations and societies was only a front for deeper issues. Each denomination was struggling to establish itself and to gain control over a given community. In this struggle for power, controversy over organizations, doctrine, theology, and procedure was only a canopy to conceal deeper motives. At this point politics and religion merge. Conversion of a community frequently meant denominational control of the local government; salvation of the individual soul was only secondary. The vicious Baptist, Methodist, and Presbyterian attacks upon Alexander Campbell's new sect, the Disciples, is a case in point. The Disciples had drawn so heavily from a Baptist group that one of its members in 1830, writes Walter Posey, attacked Campbell in the press: "If I had evidence of his being a Christian, I should call him a spiritual B____d; but that name is not appropriate. There is not a meeting-house except those of the Universalists or Unitarians that will admit him into their pulpits." Posey also relates several instances of actual sabotage against Disciples—the burning of their benches to prevent a meeting, the scheduling of meetings in conflict to prevent a large Disciple attendance, and the use of "boisterous minstrels" who sang so long that the Disciples had to wait until after twelve o'clock to begin a sermon.[36]

The Disciples did not indefinitely remain targets for abuse. By 1830 they were accepted into the fellowship of other Protestant sects who were truly "protestors" in an assault on the Catholics. Anti-Catholic feeling had existed in America from the beginning of colonization; hence, churches in the Old South merely threw up their defenses to make certain that the Pope did not extend his influence beyond the Maryland colony. The threat of Catholicism served, however, to unite Protestants on such issues as the need for missions and free Bibles to extend their influence.[37] The number of treatises from Southern presses on the subject of Roman Catholicism was far out of proportion to the threat. Yet the frontier was so torn by factionalism that outsiders were predicting success for a faith that promised unity.

Old School Presbyterians were in the forefront of the anti-Catholic crusade because they were skilled in the defense of doctrine and were perfectionists in the art of character assassination through the medium of the press. Also adept in rhetoric, Roman Catholic priests replied in kind, but gained little headway in a section which was already committed to Protestantism.

Methodists made less of a noise against Catholicism before the 1840's; however, they indulged in spreading rumors and scoffing at formalism. The mass, the worship of graven images, and excessive ritual were objects of Methodist criticism. Methodists failed in their efforts to amend the phrasing "holy catholic Church" in their Apostles' Creed, but explained that "catholic" meant strictly "universal," with no references to Romanism.

From the Baptists came sharper rebuke. Among others, editor William C. Buck pursued an aggressive attack in which he accused Catholics of espionage, sabotage, undermining the youth, and ultimate designs on American institutions.

Joseph B. Cobb in his *Mississippi Scenes* reminisced about denominational discord and strife among religionists as one Sunday morning in the 1840's he stood at a particular intersection of Church Street in Columbus. Of Methodists and Baptists he writes:

> These two . . . are the grand rival sects of the city, as indeed they are in the United States. They are ever ready for the ring, and a regular theological prize fight (not in its vulgar sense) comes off now and then between them. What is strange, too, they rarely ever contend about the essential principles of religion, but are extremely concerned to know whether the ancient prisons were provided with tan-vats, and whether the early Christians used water in Homoeopathic or Allopathic quantities. What a pity that, in order to settle this first theological proposition, the Jews or Christian fathers have not been able to excavate some manuscript remnant of Old Simon the tanner!

Then, adds Cobb, "on these important points" they are so fractious that there is "an involuntary itching to 'pitch into' each other, and take a regular Hyer and Sullivan turn."

> These rounds are sometimes pursued to a most barbarous extent. They are renewed daily for weeks at a time.
> . . . The regular ministrations of the pulpit sink into oblivion under this more absorbing and essential business, and the benches of the arena groan beneath the weight of loafers and sinners. . . . Churches . . . set apart select *champions* trained and inured to the service of theological pugilism, and it has become now as much a *science* as boxing and cudgel-playing are amongst the English. And I reverently question . . . whether St. Paul attracted larger crowds . . . than do these pulpit champions when,

betwixt the hours of exhibition, they play the *lion* on the village streets or city promenades. All honor and praise, then, to those doctrinal boxers, who distrust too much the results of Christian harmony and amalgamation to allow this *pious warfare* to become extinct! It is woefully to be dreaded that such cessation of strife might produce a most lamentable state of turpidity, from which religion could never resuscitate.[38]

Unrest and disputation flourished in the sparsely settled areas of the South. Agrarian people, not accustomed to getting to the bottom of issues, thrived on rumor and propaganda. As the country built up, the frictions and tensions subsided. Secession and the Civil War had a unifying effect, and the many differences created by sectarianism were temporarily put aside. Some of the controversies subsided, but others were revived after the war, to continue into recent times.

6

The Crusade
Against Liberalism

IF THE SECTARIAN CONFLICTS divided Southern religionists into warring groups and paved the way for the
type of militant fundamentalism characteristic of the
Bible Belt, the crusade against liberalism and sin often
united these belligerents with a feeling of self-righ-
teousness.

Divided on dogma and theology, the pulpit voiced a
solid objection to liberalism in all its varying forms, as
it resounded with the words, "Unbelief is the crying
sin!" Before 1830 there were some traces of unorthodox thinking and conduct that irritated religious leaders; but during the decades that preceded the Civil
War the ranks of the godly united against a common foe,
infidelity.

From the religious literature of the period one discovers three distinct sources of this common threat to
the Bible Belt faith: first, the deism of Thomas Paine;
second, the socialism of Robert Owen; and third, natural science. The new learning had supplied a revised
perspective of man's relation to God, the universe, nature, and the state. Although the most advanced liberalism from these three sources may appear inoffensive to
the twentieth century, it was not acceptable to most antebellum people.

Most of the liberal thought to which the pulpit objected belonged to the early portion of the nineteenth century. "Parson" Weems was found by Bishop William Meade selling Paine's *The Age of Reason* at Fairfax Courthouse.[1] In *The Freedom of Thought Struggle in the Old South*, Clement Eaton tells of a skeptical blacksmith in the Appalachians, who antagonized the laymen and whipped all the Methodist preachers journeying through his pass. One agile and muscular minister, however, "beat the hell out of him" and led him to Christ,[2] as the minister reported from the pulpit. Elihu Embree was another of the frontier deists.[3] Senator Humphrey Marshall of Kentucky; Willie Jones of North Carolina; Colonel William R. Daire, one of the founders of the University of North Carolina; Dr. David Ker, professor at the same institution; and Harris, Davies, Delvaux, Richards, and Holmes (members of the faculty) were skeptics. Others were Sir John Randolph of Williamsburg, Governor Fauquier, and George Wythe, also of the early group. At the University of Georgia was President Meigs, finally ousted by the conservative faction. Dr. Joseph Buchanan and Horace Holly, writes Niels Henry Sonne, are known for their efforts to stimulate liberalism in Transylvania University.[4] The freethinking of Thomas Jefferson, of course, is familiar to almost everyone. Albert Post explains that C. Shultz of Virginia is credited with writing *A Biblical Challenge to Bishop Hobart and Every Clergy* (1825), in which he exposed a few of the Old Testament stories without "meeting a single clergyman, who dared to risk his reputation by a denial and refutation of any of them." [5] Dr. Thomas Cooper of South Carolina College wrote articles on the origins of Christianity, "The Fabrication of the Pentateuch Proved, by the anachronisms contained in those Books," being the most celebrated. Professor James H. Thornwell, as recalled by his biographer, Benjamin M. Palmer, throws specific light on Cooper's type of skepticism:

He [Cooper] looked upon man very much as an animal, and believed that the framework of society was designed to provide for his physical wants and necessities. As in man he saw but the animal, so in the objects of nature he saw nothing but external nature. Of man in his higher nature, as a being of immortal powers, with aspirations reaching into a never ending futurity, he had no just conception.[6]

These were some of the individuals who represented the liberal approach to religion. The fact that the church did not understand their motives or the message they advocated made them suspicious characters. Although they were all worthy champions of their cause, men of intellect and social position, they were swept aside by the evangelical forces that had gained unprecedented momentum by 1830. Conservative groups joined ranks and succeeded in putting the section safely in the orthodox fold. A predominantly agrarian people, a persistent fundamentalist clergy, and inadequate low-cost educational facilities for the masses were some of the factors contributing toward making the Old South a stronghold of an emotional and orthodox faith.

When one notes the many references to infidelity in religious literature as late as 1830, he might wonder if there was not a great deal more unorthodox thinking than was actually the case. The great excitement, however, was due to the rather loose and flexible interpretation of liberalism. For instance, the terms "freethinking," "deism," "skepticism," "atheism," and "infidelity" were used synonymously in the assault upon any person or group that did not agree with the orthodox pattern. It had so long been the fashion to harangue Tom Paine, Robert Owen, and science that the pulpit had difficulty terminating the tirades. The fact that many antebellum ministers excelled in diatribes and bombast accounts for some of the attacks upon an older liberalism. Many ministers were uneducated men,

driven to cant for the want of adequate sermon materials and leisure time for study; hence they frequently
sounded off with outbursts against any belief that did
not agree with theirs.

First, there was deism, which derived its source from
the light of nature and reason. Second, there was a type
of sensationalism styled "atheism." Third, there was a
form of infidelity which the ministers called pantheism.
They attributed it to an idealistic philosophy that took
away from God his separate identity and reduced him
to a set of forces or laws within nature. Fourth, they assailed phrenology, for it pretended to make the moral
character of man dependent upon the shape of the brain
and skull. Next, the science of hypnotism or mesmerism
came in for savage treatment because it was reputed to
have the power of freeing man from his nature and
would give him the ability to perform feats beyond his
limitations. Then there was spiritualism, which appealed to those craving sensationalism, for men and
women would sit from night to night beside tables,
wrote N. L. Rice in *The Signs of the Times*, "listening
in breathless silence to certain singular raps, and spelling out, letter by letter some trifling revelation from the
spirit-world." [7] Both Universalism and Unitarianism
were among those infidelities that the pulpit looked
upon with suspect and distrust. Finally, there was an
unintellectual, unsystematized type of infidelity that
was associated with those who had doubts about their
own spiritual state. Faith was not valid unless one
knew positively the "time when" and the "place
where" his experience had occurred. Dogmatism and
faith became synonymous.

Ministers, however, were unwilling to rely entirely
upon their own sermonizing to rid the South of infidelity. They appealed particularly to the parents of young
men in colleges; they approached also the educators
themselves for support in the crusade against skep-

ticism. Education at all levels felt the influence of those who feared that the mind of youth was being contaminated.

Southern homes very early had been indoctrinated with propaganda to the effect that the state colleges were dangerous places to send the young. Parents were appealed to through open letters like the following in the *Evangelical and Literary Magazine* (1828) as to what they could do to preserve virtues and frustrate anti-Christian ideas:

(1) Let them [parents] frequently, openly, and strongly express their sentiments, on the subject of religion in Colleges. . . .

(2) Let judicious, strong, decided essays on this subject be frequently laid before the public; that the people may be enlightened, and made to see what a bearing it has on all the best interests of the commonwealth. . . .

(3) Let Christians . . . endeavor to secure the cooperation of intelligent and moral men, who, although no Christians, yet are able to see the value of religious influences on the order and peace of society. . . .

(4) Let Christians resolutely give the preference to those institutions, in which the principles of Christianity are made the basis of education: and let them show that they will in no wise countenance or support schools of any kind, where the religion of their children will be corrupted.

(5) Let all who love the cause of Christ . . . make the colleges of the country a subject of special prayer.[8]

The teaching of "the evidences of Christianity," perhaps first adopted by Timothy Dwight of Yale, was introduced into American schools to combat the irreligious and infidel impulses that grew out of the Enlightenment. All Southern institutions of any importance adopted the system, employing teachers who were specially trained to present the truths of the Bible as opposed to the skeptical concepts that were being passed around. Topics examined in the classroom included the correct use of reason in religion, the superiority of Christianity over other religions, the importance of revelation, the validity of miracles, the origin of the Bible, the prophecies, and the inspiration of the Scriptures. A very popular text was Archibald Alexander's *Evidences of the Authenticity, Inspiration, and Canonical Authority of the Holy Scriptures,* a book that was the product of his Princeton Theological Seminary lectures.

In a survey of Southern college curricula in force during the period, Orval Filbeck reveals some rather interesting material as to the dates of adopting the program and the texts used. Hampden-Sydney (Presbyterian, Virginia, founded in 1776) began the Evidences program in 1825, using Butler and Paley as texts. The University of Mississippi (founded in 1844) introduced Evidences in 1850, using Paley and Alexander; Furman University (Baptist, South Carolina, founded in 1825) introduced Evidences in 1854; Louisiana State University (founded in 1845) introduced Evidences in 1860, using Butler; Roanoke College (Lutheran, Virginia, founded in 1842) introduced Evidences in 1853, using Butler, Alexander, and Wayland; Transylvania College (originally Presbyterian but later Disciples, Kentucky, founded in 1780) introduced Evidences in 1798, using Paley and Fisher; College of Charleston (Municipal, South Carolina, founded in 1770) introduced Evidences in 1828.[9] This list cannot be complete because many antebellum schools have long since ceased to operate and their history and catalogs have been lost or destroyed by fire. But even the sample above will indicate that the Evidences movement became a popular and effective weapon against infidel philosophies.

This campaign against liberalism was not limited to pulpit, home, or college curriculum. The primary and secondary schools likewise felt that the movement indoctrinated the youthful mind with the elements of spirituality. The textbooks—primers and readers—contained a great quantity of subject matter with a religious flavor; for example, the selections for children to read had to do with the origin of the Bible, stories from the Bible, Scripture, God, Jesus Christ, pulpits, preachers, religion, immortality, heaven, creation, duty to God, the frailty of man, death, and observance of the Sabbath. From 25 to 50 percent of the total reading content was religious in sentiment. Examples of these books are the *North Carolina Reader;* Goodrich's Readers; *The Rhetorical Manual, or Southern Fifth Reader; The Southern Speaker, or Sixth Reader.*

Antebellum religionists were noted not only for their opposition to liberalism but also for their efforts to eliminate "sin" in its varying forms. The sermon literature seems to indicate that Southern minds were largely preoccupied with rescuing their neighbors from the clutches of sin. The predominance of small churches, the considerable number of agrarian folk, and the numerous uneducated preachers furnished a suitable atmosphere in which a moral crusade might flourish. "Sin" was a subject that could be discussed, challenged, and understood without too much educational background on the part of the congregation.

Pulpit protest against sin in America, however, did not have its origin in the Old South, for it began in the early seventeenth century, when the first Puritans set foot upon American soil. Increase Mather, at a meeting of ministers, "struck at the Root, speaking against mixed Dances." [10] In his *Arrow Against Profane and Promiscuous Dancing* he writes, "Is this a time for *Jigs* and *Galiards!*" Again, in his *Testimony Against Several Profane and Superstitious Customs,* Mather shows the immoralities of "Stage-Plays" and the "barbaric paganism involved in setting up a may-pole." He likewise assails "Health drinking." "An Health," he says, "is that which doth Oblige men to Drink such a quantity of liquor, as an Indication of their Praying for the Health or Prosperity of such a Person, or of such a Design." Mather also writes that people should abstain from gambling, and he condemns Christmas celebrations because they keep alive a pagan festival flavored with Catholicism.[11] Methodist objection to the luxuries of dress may even have a precedent in the Puritans' opposition to "Red coats and gold lace," which to them were violations of public morals. Antebellum scorn of too much amusement may also have orginated in early Puritan objection to cockfighting, gaiety, and various types of frivolities.

The eighteenth century, likewise, did not look with favor upon excessive entertainment. For example, Timothy Dwight, although participating briefly in student functions, recognized the evils of too much fun. He discouraged balls and dancing, and was opposed to unlawful games and billiards. He lamented that in their reading, girls usually "sink down to songs, novels, and plays." [12] His society regarded such frivolous reading as fatal because the mind of youth was introduced to a world totally unlike anything in everyday life. Orthodox religionists throughout New England reacted similarly to the many so-called evils of the day.

Nineteenth-century America, too, had definite views about morals. Thomas L. Nichols observes: "In the estimation of the pious, most of the pleasures, amusements, and recreations of life were sinful. It was a sin to dance, or even to play a dancing tune, but right enough to play marches. A quick step would pass muster, but not a horn pipe or jig." [13] Card-playing was looked upon as wicked even when there was no gambling, but a game of draughts or fox and geese was permissible. Billiards or ninepins, however, were not sanctioned by the pious. Around the turn of the century many people

drank rum, brandy, and cider; in fact, even the early circuit and itinerant preachers along the frontier felt that
not to take a "swig" from the family jug was a breach of
etiquette.[14] But when drunkenness became more common, temperance reform sprang up, and it "was carried
out so unsparingly that spirits were banished, the apple
orchards cut down to prevent the making of cider,
'Maine Laws' were finally passed, and drinking any in-
toxicating beverage, ever so temperately, was thought a
sin of such magnitude as to justify excommunication." [15]
On Sunday no traveling was allowed, and attempts
were made to stop government mails on the Sabbath.
Among the staunch religionists no music was tolerated
except church music, and recreation of any kind was
frowned upon by the devout. In America after revivalism had made its influence felt, all was solemn and
drear, with laughter considered irreverent. Nichols
writes: "There was a ban upon everything like mirth,
pleasure, festivity on all days, but especially on Sunday.
Life was too earnest and solemn a thing, and eternity
too terrible, according to the Calvinistic theology, to
allow of jollity, or any but the most serious happiness." [16]

From the preceding, one can see that Southerners
came by their objection to sin naturally enough. Their
antipathy for waywardness, as defined by an evangelical faith, seemed to take on the characteristics of a crusade. Sermons of Methodist, Baptist, Disciples of
Christ, and sometimes Presbyterian ministers were con-
spicuous for their concern over drinking, the use of tobacco, card-playing, and at least a dozen other so-called
vices. State legislatures passed bills prohibiting blasphemy, atheism, Sabbath-breaking, polygamy, and similar violations of general Christian morality, as in-
terpreted by the nineteenth century. Society formulated
a set of moral attitudes which have come to be associated with the South of somewhat recent times.

Following in the wake of the Great Revival and paralleling the great denominational controversies over doctrine and the attack upon liberalism came the period that from all appearances was a moral crusade. Perhaps the most frequently discussed topic was that of drinking spirituous liquor, with all its multitudinous evils. The campaign against the use of tobacco was well organized. The evils of dancing, playing cards, and attending amusement centers like the theater and the circus were material for the moralists. Ministers also objected to fictitious narratives, novels, impure sentimental poetry, and certain types of biographies because they did not give an accurate picture of life and produced a morbid cultivation of the feelings and sensibilities. Political newspapers, fashionable monthlies, and popular weeklies were considered by many to be in bad taste for consumption by a family group. Other vices which became the raw materials for many sermons were the following: Sunday newspapers, fighting, dueling, brawling, quarreling, profane swearing, divorce, violation of the marriage relation, seduction, incest, fornication, polygamy, excessive luxuries, unethical legal operations, usury, gossiping, and Sabbath-breaking.

Although Southerners might be unable to agree on a method of eradicating these vices, they were united in support of their spiritual leaders. A type of religious solidarity was achieved, and Southern evangelicals offered a united front against a common foe—"sin," in its manifold disguises. This type of religiousness directed its attention toward moral perfection, developing a hostility toward all those who violated the code of the churches. In the process it lost sight of larger problems such as the implications of slavery. However, the emphasis upon moralism may have been the outgrowth of evangelical Christianity's inability to deal with a really critical economic and political problem. To the twentieth century the crusades against liberalism and sin might appear to have been merely a face-saving maneuver.

7

Modern Survivals
of the Camp Meeting

A HUNDRED YEARS have seen many changes. In a rural
setting, however, in which the need for spiritual sustenance and fellowship is dear to human hearts, people
change slowly. Although the circuit rider has dismounted and his type of faith is no longer in flower,
there are still traces of this older religiousness in the
twentieth century.

This book until now has been primarily concerned
with the roots of Southern piety. There are still a few of
an earlier generation, now in their twilight years, who
may have feelings of nostalgia as they peruse these
pages. They have lived through the gradual phasing out
of this earlier type of religiousness. They will recognize
that the second half of the nineteenth century carried
on the tradition and that there are evidences of this earlier behavior and thought in the twentieth. For example, Charles Drake in his *Pioneer Life in Kentucky*
captures the tone of all such reminiscences, as he exam-
ines with some degree of sentiment these transitional
years. He remembers with considerable emotion "the
bright and cheerful Sabbath mornings, which were to
the children like the daily sunshine of an hour, through
some opening in the thick leaves of the woods, to the
little blossoms below." Sunday was to him a day of rest
from the hard labors of the field; yet it was not a time

for idleness, with the stock to be cared for and the many household duties to be performed before going to church. It was a day for dressing up in one's best apparel. Only a boy who has toiled during the week in coarse dirty clothes, adds Drake, can appreciate the effect of a clean face and feet, a clean shirt, and store-bought clothes.[1]

Those familiar with rural life in the South around the turn of the century recognize remnants of their own childhood in Drake's account. The author of this book can recall reports of the Sunday morning routine. Every member of the household discharged duties with the precision of a workman on a factory assembly line. In anticipation of the moment of the family's departure for church, even the hound dogs assumed an air of officiousness by excessive barking and nipping at chickens idly standing in their way.

Mother in her calico dress, a black silk bonnet tied beneath her chin with a piece of narrow ribbon, hardly suggested that person who had baked, scrubbed, and ironed on Saturday. Father, his shoes blackened with soot and hog lard mixed together, in his special Sunday coat, a slightly worn hat on his head, a bandanna handkerchief visible in his pocket, certainly did not resemble the weather-beaten figure who on the day before had plowed from sunup to dusk in the stubborn black waxy soil of northeastern Texas—indeed a Southerner by all the criteria established in these pages. He had the stern countenance of one whose activities and destiny were determined by the unpredictable elements. The oldest son of around twelve years, a man when it came to work but only a boy at heart, had already hitched the team to the buckboard and had placed behind the newly acquired spring-seat cane-bottom chairs for himself and his brothers and sisters—a perilous arrangement because they had been known to tip over backwards with a sudden lurch forward by the team.

His fustian jacket and hat brushed for the occasion were almost a disguise. On his stubbed and festered toe was a new rag, but such minor physical discomforts were numbed by the gladness of anticipation. Already he could visualize the horses tied along the fence, the people shaking hands and inquiring about health and crop conditions (the principal topics of rural conversation), some strolling among the graves, and all the children sitting on the grass waiting for the parson to give the sign for everyone to file into the church, the exterior of which was constructed from unfinished pine siding. Even at the moment of reminiscences this lad could feel the hard benches (some of which, in the rear, were without backs—designed for the Negro laborer who might come along to glean a few spiritual crumbs); he could hear his father's voice in the choir as it challenged all others on the confidence-invoking words:

"Amazing grace! How sweet the sound
That saved a wretch like me!
I once was lost but now am found,
Was blind, but now I see."

He could feel the resonance of the preacher's voice as he uttered the final "Amen" that terminated a prayer sometimes of a ten-minute duration, which included almost everything in the boy's experience, from salvation to boll weevil control. As the congregation filed into the sunshine, he recalled their voices against the background of birds singing in the trees and the animals shaking their harnesses. Then remembering that this was the day for quarterly conference, he could smell the aroma of fried chicken and custard pies coming from the many baskets prepared for the ceremony—"dinner on the grounds." Such were the visions that kept his spirit alive during the week in the hours of loneliness as he plowed the long rows of cotton. This lad, the symbolic grandfather of today's youth, might not be able to understand the ideological conflicts of our day but he nurtured the only values he knew. He shared in the painful struggle of his parents to survive, and firmly believed that the world and mankind were good. He had his dreams—unsophisticated—but dreams nevertheless.

A few Southerners now alive can remember J. B. Culpepper, the Methodist circuit rider in Georgia, who could appropriately be referred to as "the man in the pulpit." Then someone is sure to ask, "What about J.B.'s son Burke?" By the age of eight, Burke had learned enough from his father to fill a pulpit, and soon was spoken of as "the Boy Preacher." In 1899, at the age of nineteen, young Burke was licensed to preach by the Methodist Episcopal Church, South. According to William G. McLoughlin, Jr., he was an admirer of Sam Jones and in 1906 was considered to be "the Sam Jones of today." Later he came to be regarded as the "Billy Sunday of the South." [2]

In the summer of 1924, the author of these pages recalls, Burke Culpepper held a two-week revival meeting in Bonham, Texas, on a large plot of ground adjoining the First Methodist Church. The title of one of his evening sermons was "Killing Big Dogs." As he paced back and forth in front of the footlights, he glared at every boy and girl sitting on the front rows. For some reason the parents always chose to be farther back. As he pounded his open palm with a book of revival hymns, rolled up in the shape of a club, his nostrils, to those who were hypnotized by his homely imagery, seemed to exude both smoke and flame. Frothing at the mouth, so it seemed to the small folk trapped there in the front rows harboring their young guilt, which they were being acquainted with, he lunged first to the right and then to the left of the platform swinging his simulated club so violently that these victims feared he would "kill the little dogs" also. He shouted and gritted his teeth angrily, shook his head and snorted, crouched and lurched forward as if he were engaged in a hand-to-hand combat with an invisible opponent. Half an hour later, after the choir had sung the last stanza of "Softly and Tenderly" several times, the chorus was repeated over and over:

"Come home, come home, Ye who are weary, come home!
Earnestly, tenderly, Jesus is calling,
 Calling, O sinner, come home!"

With each appeal four or five more persons joined the deadly serious group already assembled before the platform. Culpepper stood quietly on the steps of the platform with arms outstretched, as quiet as a burned-out volcano. His tear-stained cheeks and soft, pleading voice now dispelled young fears, and the panic-stricken victims who had hovered together as if for protection an hour earlier now wanted to walk forward and shake his hand and join the throng being quietly interviewed by members of Culpepper's troupe.

These children felt only the flood of emotion. Their parents believed him to be a messenger from God. No one viewed him philosophically or historically as a legacy to the Bible Belt from evangelical Christianity, a stereotype of one who one hundred years earlier had ridden the gospel trail. Whoever he was and whatever he achieved, one thing is certain—he was an actor and a showman who put vaudeville into the old-time religion.

In the West and Southwest there have been a few preachers during the past fifty years who have ridden the gospel trail as did those men in antebellum days, perhaps substituting an old model automobile for the horse and saddlebags. Some years ago Ralph Hall, a young-looking, gray-haired ex-cowhand from Texas, closely resembled in method and physique the "knights of the saddle" such as Peter Cartwright and Lorenzo Dow. Hall, wrote Oren Arnold, has delivered religion on the hoof to perhaps a greater number of persons in a more sparsely settled country than any circuit rider before him. His circuit extended from the Mississippi River to the Pacific Ocean and from Canada to Mexico. His followers included those people on isolated farms and ranches who still had a hankering for the old-fashioned religion. He was greeted with the same type of hospitality common in the Old South. When he paid his annual visit to the Morton family, who lived seventy miles from either telephone or post office, he could expect a heartwarming reception. Mother Morton would come running toward Hall whooping, "Law-w-w-w me! If it ain't Brother Hall! I'll have a chicken on cooking in no time at all!" As she spoke she would stoop and grab a fryer with a "hawk-like suddenness" and have its neck wrung and tossed to the dog before she reached the preacher to throw her arms around him.

His normal technique was to arrive on the farm or ranch when there was considerable work to be done; then he would join in to help with anything that was in progress—the herding, the branding, or the dehorning of cattle. He worked with the people by day and talked about Jesus at night around the campfire or from an improvised pulpit—the back end of a chuck wagon or cattle truck, maybe a stump or a log. His adaptability and sincerity endeared him to the thousands who eagerly awaited his visits.

Once on a visit to the Mortons he preached a sermon out in the front yard under an oak tree. When he finished his discourse about the middle of the morning, a man stood up and said, "Since we haven't seen you in months, Brother Hall, and won't see you likely for several months again, and the day's not more'n half started yet, would it be ongrateful if we just asked you to take and preach another sermon to us now?" So Hall gave them another discourse before dinner. Following the meal, he preached a funeral sermon for a baby who had died since his last visit; then he christened an infant. After these ceremonies he was requested to preach especially for the young people, but still the gathering refused to disband. So after a bit of silence an old lady stood up from her quilt on the hard ground and spoke hesitantly to the folk around her, "I don't mean to be selfish, but ef it ain't being too brash, and ef nobody else don't want nothing, and ef Brother Hall ain't plumb tuckered out, why it ain't nothing on earth I'd ruther do right now than to listen to another sermon." And without hesitation the obliging circuit rider climbed back up on the wagon and delivered his fourth message, holding on until sundown.[3] Here we have a modern version of antebellum dedication and devotion to a people waiting to hear a simple gospel. This is the type of religiousness that characterized the latter half of the nineteenth century.

One of the most popular of the traditional modern evangelists is the Baptist preacher Billy Graham, whose weekly radio broadcast *The Hour of Decision* is carried by 975 stations, and whose filmed crusades for Christ are used by several hundred television stations. In his earlier ministry he resurrected something of the enthusiasm of the late Billy Sunday and drew crowds reminiscent of the mammoth outdoor meetings at Cane Ridge. The fundamental difference, however, is the absence of weeping and shouting, with less emphasis on hell. He talks about the human drama—doubts, fears, loneliness when man separates himself from God.[4] The solution to all problems is a simple faith and acceptance of Jesus as the personal Savior. He is less of the entertainer than was Sunday. There is no breaking of collapsible chairs across the pulpit, no leaping high into the air as if to catch a baseball, or standing on his head. He seems not to strive for undue excitement among those who are affected by his message. He speaks to the individual and masses everywhere. Since his crusades abroad, one will detect a sort of internationalism in his utterances.

Graham speaks to large audiences. Early in his ministry he addressed 40,000 people in the football stadium at the University of South Carolina, where several thousand filed down from the stands to make their commitment.[5] On June 1, 1952, the author of these pages began collecting eyewitness information at a Graham meeting at Houston, Texas, where 60,000 gathered under the stars in the new football stadium on the Rice Institute (now William Marsh Rice University) campus. A crowd of 70,000 had been expected for the finale of his series of thirty-three services, but rain and an overcast sky reduced the attendance to 45,000. Roy Rogers and Dale Evans were added attractions with their testimonies. The size of a Graham audience is almost determined by the capacity of the auditorium or stadium. In Houston's Astrodome, 61,000 joined the late President Lyndon B. Johnson and Mrs. Johnson on November 28, 1965, a crowd that seemed to have assembled for a variety of reasons. The New York services in Madison Square Garden and Yankee Stadium, where some 2,397,000 heard Graham, brought forth 61,000 who made decisions. As for spectacle, his international crusades even dwarf those in the United States.

Relying almost entirely upon personal magnetism, Graham casts a spell upon everyone within the sound of his voice. For example, in one of the Houston meetings feelings ran unusually high as thousands filed out of the stands onto the gridiron with each appeal. A Unitarian minister who attended these services four times in one week responded that he felt the spell and was "hypnotized by the chanting music, influenced by the suggestions, the will of the crowd to believe anything."

Houstonians either accepted Billy Graham or recognized his right to portray this older type of religiousness. However, as during the antebellum period, there were echoes of controversy as public objection was registered. For instance, one minister, attacking Graham from the pulpit, stated: "To me, it is like feeding a starving man sawdust. The sawdust stills the pangs of hunger, but the victim dies as everyone does physically and spiritually without nourishing food." He went on to point out that Graham sees nothing but evil in the world and his thinking is marked by half-truths. Graham prefers "Jesus to Freud, Jesus to Sociology, Jesus to Psychology, Jesus to Politics." That is, there is no comparison, only one choice. Later in his attack on Graham, he added: "One can have the spirit of Jesus and believe the teachings of Freud, practice psychology, study sociology, and delve into politics. The spirit of Jesus . . . is not exclusive; it is inclusive." Reinhold Niebuhr stated this objection cogently when he faulted Graham for his simple answers to complex questions.[6] Thus, as in the earlier religious expressions, hostility arose when emotionalism replaced the more rational approach.

Graham appears to be something of an enigma to those who see him only as a one-dimensional personality, but like the earlier circuit riders he reflects a versatility that the casual critics do not recognize. The complexities of the times have compelled him to move in a variety of settings—from the White House to the ghettos, from the intellectualism of college campuses to the anti-intellectualism of many of the lower middle class, from the more formal atmosphere of the symphony hall to the informal "rock festivals." Yet wherever he performs he maintains that his message is the same. "My approach," he says, "is simple and direct." Holding an open Bible, he adds: "The Gospel in my hands becomes a hammer and a flame!" Although his ultimate concern is "the cosmic struggle between Christ and Satan" [7] as it affects personal salvation, he has added race, war, and the moral crises of the times to his sermon material, whereas the circuit preacher referred to man's ills in terms of a rigid moralistic code.

In Denver, Colorado, on June 3, 1970, Graham entered the controversy between black militants and the church to answer the accusation that Southern Baptists had "castrated, murdered, and raped" Negroes. He said that "the church as the church is not guilty. But some members of several churches may have done that in the past to our shame and deep sorrow." On the issue of the youth revolt he conceded that students are making legitimate appeals for the reform of education in America. "Young people are asking religious questions and . . . universities are not answering those fundamental gut-level questions young people are asking." He attacked, however, the youthful protesters who engage in violence, disrupt order, and deny a hearing to those who oppose their views. "Everyone from Stokely Carmichael to Vice-President Agnew ought to be able to have their say." He has been critical of the radical students "who want to tear the country down but have no plan to put in its place." On the controversial subject of abortion laws in the United States he pointed out instances when he favored permitting abortion—in cases of rape, incest, and where the life of the mother is in danger. On the topic of birth control he was direct, saying that he had no objection "because sex within marriage is for enjoyment as well as procreation." [8]

During the thirty years of his evangelical career he has preached almost everywhere and discussed most of mankind's problems, his solutions remaining essentially the same. "Jesus," he says, "is the answer." Here again Billy Graham is in tune with the clerics of antebellum days, offering a solution that might appear both ambiguous and evasive, as the critics of the earlier era proclaimed. As in the nineteenth century, such solutions are viewed by some as a sedative or a narcotic, a type of faith that pleases those who subscribe to an uncritical acceptance of the American way. Graham's most severe critics refer to him as a "Pied Piper, leading a deluded people into the swamps of ancient superstition," [9] or as a White House guru, from the administration of Eisenhower to that of Nixon.

Another in a long line of evangelists who have come over the Cumberland Gap to bring the gospel to frontier and mountain people is Grady Wilson, like Graham a graduate of Wheaton College in Illinois, and a member of the Graham organization since 1947. Sid Moody of the *Atlanta Journal and Constitution* staff describes a two-week revival meeting in the summer of 1966 at Harlan, Kentucky, conducted by Wilson and his assistants Arne Robertson, evangelist and choir director, and Ted Cornell, organist and pianist, a graduate of Juilliard School of Music.

As in the early days, there were those who did not approve of evangelism and its techniques. Just as the circuit rider came under rebuke, so did Wilson. "Grady was repeating his jokes," said one, "and his emotionalism was an insult to people's intelligence." "He was proof," said another minister, "that old-time religion was old-time religion."

Grady Wilson, though, was student enough of the American scene to know that the religious life wears many faces. Wilson knew where he was, and when he cried "repent and be saved" he knew that the people heard and understood. Their hearts were still as responsive as their great-grandparents'. Wilson explains his approach and the basis of his appeal:

> The difference between the evangelical and liturgical church depends on cultural background, esthetics, taste. The essential thing is proclamation of God's good news to the world. Our tradition is evangelical. Our life, our tastes are based on an agrarian culture. They are simpler than those of an urban society. The prayer meeting here is religious but it is also social. It's a chance for the peo-

ple from one hollow to see the folks up another hollow. In Appalachia, people do not take to change readily. If it meets their needs, they stay with something. Historically, change to our people has meant exploitation.

He admitted that they were not doing anything new. "I put in topical references to the time, to Kentucky, but the gospel is relevant to the world, now, at this hour. It never changes."

Resistance to change characterizes the old-time evangelical Christianity. One hundred and fifty years earlier Peter Cartwright had expounded the theme "No Time for God" in almost the same place. Grady Wilson concluded one of his sermons with the same warning of the imminence of death:

In Harlan County, you have time for education, time for business, time for the Chamber of Commerce, but have you had time for God? One of these days you are going to have to die because you have no lease on life. Open your hearts to Jesus before it's too late. One of these nights your race of life will be over. The grave will be opened. Your casket may already be in town. I don't know. But are you ready to die? Are you ready to leave this beautiful stadium before saying 'yes' to Jesus Christ? This may be the night for which you were born into the world. Everyone here tonight is going to make a choice in a few minutes: to accept Christ or to leave Him.[10]

This author is familiar with most of the twentieth-century counterparts of the "old-time religion," those ranging from a deep, sentimental seriousness to the more offbeat orgies that characterize the dead end of fundamentalism. Some of these groups give the traveler across the Southland special warnings with their road signs on hairpin curves or near narrow bridges— "Prepare to Meet God!" "The End Is Near!" "Jesus Saves!"

H. L. Mencken, when he was at Dayton, Tennessee,

reporting the famous Scopes trial for the *American Mercury*, accompanied by a newspaperwoman, wrote an essay entitled "The Hills of Zion," in which he depicts this type of fundamentalism. His portrayal of these mountain people near Morgantown is reminiscent of many of the antebellum festivals already reviewed. Mencken's critics, like those of Sinclair Lewis (*Elmer Gantry*), charged that a blow had been dealt "below the Bible Belt."

Mencken wrote as follows:

Far off in a dark, romantic glade a flickering light was visible, and out of the silence came the rumble of exhortation. We could distinguish the figure of the preacher only as a moving mote in the light: it was like looking down the tube of a dark-field microscope. Slowly and cautiously we crossed what seemed to be a pasture, and then we crouched down along the edge of a cornfield, and stealthily edged further and further. The light now grew larger and we could begin to make out what was going on. We went ahead on all fours, like snakes in the grass.

From the great limb of a mighty oak hung a couple of crude torches of the sort that car inspectors thrust under Pullman cars when a train pulls in at night. In the guttering glare was the preacher, and for a while we could see no one else. He was an immensely tall and thin mountaineer in blue jeans, his collarless shirt open at the neck and his hair a tousled mop. As he preached he paced up and down under the smoking flambeaux, and at each turn he thrust his arms into the air and yelled "Glory to God!" We crept nearer in the shadow of the cornfield, and began to hear more of his discourse. He was preaching on the Day of Judgment. The high kings of the earth, he roared, would all fall down and die; only the sanctified would stand up to receive the Lord God of Hosts. One of these kings he mentioned by name, the king of what he called Greece-y. The king of Greece-y, he said, was doomed to hell. We crawled forward a few more yards and began to see the audience. It was seated on benches ranged around the preacher in a circle. Behind him sat a row of elders, men and women. In front were the younger folk. We crept on cautiously, and individuals rose out of the ghostly gloom. A young mother sat suckling her baby, rocking as the preacher paced up and down. Two scared little girls hugged each other, their pigtails down their backs. An immensely huge mountain woman, in a gingham dress, cut in one piece, rolled on her heels at every "Glory to God!" To one side, and but half visible, was what appeared to be a bed. We found afterward that half a dozen babies were asleep upon it.

The preacher stopped at last, and there arose out of the darkness a woman with her hair pulled back into a little tight knot. She began so quietly that we couldn't hear what she said, but soon her voice rose resonantly and we could follow her. She was denouncing the reading of books. Some wandering book agent, it appeared, had come to her cabin and tried to sell her a specimen of his wares. She refused to touch it. Why, indeed, read a book? If what was in it was true, then everything in it was already in the Bible. If it was false, then reading it would imperil the soul. This syllogism from Caliph Omar complete, she sat down. There followed a hymn, led by a somewhat fat brother wearing silver-rimmed country spectacles. It droned on for half a dozen stanzas and then the first speaker resumed the floor. He argued that the gift of tongues was real and that education was a snare. Once his children could read the Bible, he said, they had enough. Beyond lay only infidelity and damnation. Sin stalked the cities. Dayton itself was a Sodom. Even Morgantown had begun to forget God. He sat down, and a female aurochs in gingham got up. She began quietly, but was soon leaping and roaring, and it was hard to follow her. Under the cover of the turmoil we sneaked a bit closer.

A couple of other discourses followed, and there were two or three hymns. Suddenly a change of mood began to make itself felt. The last hymn ran longer than the others, and dropped gradually into a monotonous, unintelligible chant. The leader beat time with his book. The faithful broke out with exultations. When the singing ended there was a brief palaver that we could not hear, and two of the men moved a bench into the circle of light directly under the flambeaux. Then a half-grown girl emerged from the darkness and threw herself upon it. We noticed with astonishment that she had bobbed hair. "This sister," said the leader, "has asked for prayers." We moved a bit closer. We could now see faces plainly, and hear every word. What followed quickly reached such heights of barbaric grotesquerie that it was hard to believe it real. At a signal all the faithful crowded up to the bench and began to pray—not in unison, but each for himself! At another they all fell on their knees, their arms over the penitent. The leader kneeled facing us, his head alternately thrown back dramatically or buried in his hands. Words spouted from his lips like bullets from a machine-gun—appeals to God to pull the penitent back out of hell, defiances of the demons of the air, a vast impassioned jargon of apocalyptic texts. Suddenly he rose to his feet, threw back his head and began to speak in the tongues—blub-blub-blub, gurgle-gurgle-gurgle. His voice rose to a higher register. The climax was a shrill, inarticulate squawk, like that of a man throttled. He fell headlong across the pyramid of supplicants.

A comic scene? Somehow, no. The poor halfwits were too horribly in earnest. It was like peeping through a knothole at the writhings of people in pain. From the squirming and jabbering mass a young woman gradually detached herself—a woman not uncomely, with a pathetic homemade cap on her head. Her head jerked back, the veins of her neck swelled, and her fists went to her throat as if she were fighting for breath. She bent backward until she was like half a hoop. Then she suddenly snapped forward. We caught a flash of the whites of her eyes. Presently her whole body began to be convulsed— great throes that began at the shoulders and ended at the hips. She would leap to her feet, thrust her arms in air, and then hurl herself upon the heap. Her praying flattened out into a more delirious caterwauling, like that of a Tom cat on a petting party. I describe the thing discreetly, and as a strict behaviorist. The lady's subjective sensations I leave to infidel pathologists, privy to the works of Ellis, Freud, and Moll. Whatever they were, they were obviously not painful, for they were accompanied by vast heavings and gurglings of a joyful and even ecstatic nature. And they seemed to be contagious, too, for soon a second penitent, also female, joined the first, and then came a third, and a fourth, and a fifth. The last one had an extraordinary violent attack. She began with mild enough jerks of the head, but in a moment she was bounding all over the place, like a chicken with its head cut off. Every time her head came up a stream of hosannas would issue out of it. Once she collided with a dark, undersized brother, hitherto silent and stolid. Contact with her set him off as if he had been kicked by a mule. He leaped into the air, threw back his head, and began to gargle as if with a mouthful of BB shot. Then he loosed one tremendous stentorian sentence in the tongues, and collapsed.

By this time the performers were quite oblivious to the profane universe and so it was safe to go still closer. We left our hiding and came up to the little circle of light. We slipped into the vacant seats on one of the rickety benches. The heap of mourners was directly before us. They bounced into us as they cavorted. The smell that they radiated, sweating there in that obscene heap, half suffocated us. Not all of them, of course, did the thing in the grand manner. Some merely moaned and rolled their eyes. The female ox in gingham flung her great bulk on the ground and jabbered an unintelligible prayer. One of the men, in the intervals between fits, put on his spectacles and read his Bible. Beside me on the bench sat the young mother and her baby. She suckled it through the whole orgy, obviously fascinated by what was going on, but never venturing to take any hand in it. On the bed just outside the light half a dozen other babies slept peacefully. In the shadows, suddenly appearing and as suddenly going away, were vague figures, whether of believers or of scoffers I do not know. They seemed to come and go in couples. Now and then a couple at the ringside would step out and vanish into the black night. After a while some came back, the males looking somewhat sheepish. There was whispering outside the circle of vision. A couple of Fords lurched up the road, cutting holes in the darkness with their lights. Once some one out of sight loosed a bray of laughter.

All this went on for an hour or so. The original penitent, by this time, was buried three deep beneath the heap. One caught a glimpse, now and then, of her yellow bobbed hair, but then she would vanish again. How she breathed down there I don't know; it was hard enough six feet away, with a strong five-cent cigar to help. When the praying brothers would rise up for a bout with the tongues their faces were streaming with perspiration. The fat harridan in gingham sweated like a longshoreman. Her hair got loose and fell down over her face. She fanned herself with her skirt. A powerful old gal she was, plainly equal in her day to a bout with obstetrics and a week's washing on the same morning, but this was worse than a week's washing. Finally, she fell into a heap, breathing in great, convulsive gasps.

Finally, we got tired of the show and returned to Dayton.[11]

If time had permitted, Mencken could have driven through the Southland during the months of July and August and found replicas of the older camp meetings, much more refined than the one he observed. Perhaps one of the largest is the Methodist camp at Indian Springs, Georgia, where the tabernacle has a seating capacity of 5,000. This plant was organized by a Reverend Mr. Dodge of the North Georgia conference. Other Methodist camps include the one at Hartselle, Alabama; the site at Frost Bridge, Mississippi; camps at Summit, Mississippi; Carrollton, Georgia; Wilmore, Kentucky; Corbin, Kentucky; Locust Grove, Georgia; Waycross, Georgia; and Dixon's Mill near Thomaston, Alabama. The Little Texas camp near Tuskegee is perhaps the oldest in Alabama, organized in 1866. The tabernacle still stands, but the original cottages are gone. Black, Alabama, has probably the best of the new and smaller camps. It was organized in 1928 by the Vanlandingham brothers and W. J. Hughes, their brother-in-law—all members of the Alabama Methodist conference. It has a tabernacle with a seating capacity of 2,000. The Nazarenes have a site at Millport, Alabama, which was purchased from the Methodists. Their tabernacle, about fifty years old, has a seating capacity of 2,200; the campgrounds will provide for 1,500. Other Nazarene establishments are at Bradenton and Lakeland, Florida. Here and at the many other meeting places dotting the countryside one can still see only slightly modified versions of antebellum Christianity in the out-of-doors.

8
Sensationalism and Excesses

SOME OF THE SENSATIONALISM of the antebellum camp meetings finds expression in those religious services where snake-handling and faith healing are involved. On the plantations before the Civil War, healing cults were informally organized with the voodoo specialist as the central figure. Conditioned by the miracles of the Scriptures, religionists continued to believe in what many today would consider unscientific phenomena. Expecting and demanding magic, religious cults are not strange to contemporary America. They flourish particularly when a small minority from the same culture band together in search of happiness, or a quick cure to ills, or solutions to problems that society may have caused and for which it thus far appears to have no ready remedy.

The introduction of snake-handling and faith healing has given a new twist to old-fashioned camp meetings. Cults participating in snake-handling attracted the attention of the press as early as the 1930's in Kentucky, Virginia, and Tennessee. These continue to exist despite statutes forbidding the practice of snake-handling. Since there is a Biblical promise that poisonous serpents will do no harm to the faithful, the laws are defied. Perhaps as many as 300,000 persons in the South belong to these "holiness" cults, and they are motivated by a deep religious emotion. As a rule, they are without education and belong to the lowest income groups. They are also remarkable for their fanaticism, submitting to snakebites and the hazards of drinking poison to test their faith. In the meetings of these cults, as in the camp meetings of the late eighteenth century and the early nineteenth century, religious "exercises" such as swooning, paroxysms, jumping, furious dancing, boisterous behavior, or speaking in tongues are common.

In 1947, according to John A. Womeldorf, writing in *The Christian Century*, among the most famous of the snake handlers was Bill Parsons, leader of a small religious sect near Stone Creek, Virginia, known as the Holiness Faith Healers. Their "Shrine of Divine Healing," or "Church of the Snake Handlers," was referred to in magazines and newspapers more than one hundred times during the 1930's. By 1947, at the time of Womeldorf's writing, "Little George" Hensley of Pineville, Kentucky, had been participating in the ritual for thirty-five years and had received more than 250 snake bites.

Perhaps the keynoter for these cults, as reported by Womeldorf, was a K. D. Browning of the Pine Mountain section of Kentucky, who used Mark 16:17–18 as a frequent text: "And these signs shall follow them that believe; In my name shall they cast out devils; they shall speak with new tongues; They shall take up serpents; and if they drink any deadly thing, it shall not hurt them; they shall lay hands on the sick, and they shall recover." Also Luke 10:19: "Behold, I give unto you power to tread on serpents and scorpions, and over all the power of the enemy; and nothing shall by any means hurt you." Or Jer. 8:17: "For, behold, I will send serpents, cockatrices, among you, which will not be charmed, and they shall bite you, saith the LORD."

The mountain people observe practices and rituals

very much like those which characterized the early camp meetings. For instance:

> On the third Saturday and Sunday of each month the mountain folk would bring large baskets of food for meetings that lasted all day and most of the night as well. Hour after hour the wooded hillsides resounded with clanging cymbals, shouting, hand-clapping, and primitive singing that might have reminded one of the voodoos of the jungle. After an orgy of emotional manifestations, one of the cultists would feel the spirit upon him and, taking up a writhing serpent, would wrap it round his neck or fondle it in his arms. Snakes were passed from hand to hand in an atmosphere that fairly crackled with nervous tension. Quite frequently the snakes sank their fangs into the flesh of the handlers, but faith would usually make them whole again. If not, better was it for a person to die "atrusting in the Lord" than to live in sin by having the devil send one of his doctors to effect a cure.[1]

The handling of snakes usually occurs against the background of ecclesiastical jazz. Guitar music and old revival tunes such as "The Devil in a Box," "Wicked Polly," and "Ring Them Bells of Love," observes Womeldorf, accelerate in emotions until the cultists begin an incessant clapping of hands and shoutings of "sweet Jesus," interspersed with screams in an unknown tongue. The introduction of snakes and the passing of them from hand to hand sends the emotions to a higher level. Madness seems to grip some as they take off their shoes and walk barefoot on the serpents.

Participating in these séances are certain minor sects of the South, Holiness and Church of God groups, for example, in Kentucky, Tennessee, Virginia, Florida, Alabama, North Carolina—wherever snakes and primitive and impoverished folk abound. However, such cults also exist in the Midwest, Southwest, and West. They are a legacy of the old-time emotionalism.

A forerunner of the faith healers who toured the South was Aimee Semple McPherson, a Canadian evangelist, who established the International Church of the Foursquare Gospel in Los Angeles in 1927. She introduced such spectaculars as riding into the church on a white horse wearing regal flowing robes and brandishing a flaming torch. With churches in all sections of the United States, this group holds beliefs essentially Protestant and Trinitarian, with special emphasis upon divine healing. Acceptance of the sacraments of Baptism and the Lord's Supper and expectation of the Second Coming of Christ to earth reveal a kinship to many Christian groups.

Two religious bodies have a primary emphasis upon healing and health: the Church of Christ, Scientist, and the Divine Science movement. The following also report an emphasis upon healing as a part of their doctrine: The Church of Jesus Christ of Latter-day Saints, the Reorganized Church of Jesus Christ of Latter Day Saints, the Churches of God, the evangelistic associations, the Pentecostal Assemblies, the Holiness Churches, and the Church of the Nazarene. Apart from the evangelistic sects, the Anglican communion (in America, the Episcopal Church) has taken an interest in faith healing, and with the realization that many bodily ills are psychosomatic The United Methodist Church has begun to feel that religion may have an answer to certain problems that internal medicine cannot reach. The First Presbyterian Church in Pittsburgh has opened its doors to Kathryn Kuhlman every Friday morning, when she performs her faith healing before an overflow gathering, including physicians and clergy. A spectator from Bakersfield, California, watched her perform in a West Coast service and spoke of her as "the greatest thing since Christ!" [2]

Oral Roberts, tall and rangy Oklahoman, became identified with faith healing in 1935, when he was seventeen years old. Suffering from tuberculosis and plagued by stuttering from early childhood, according to his autobiography, he was being carried by his parents and older brother Elmer to a meeting conducted by a Rev. George Moncey. His brother had bought gasoline for the trip with his last thirty-five cents and had helped put Oral on a mattress on the back seat of the car. En route to the service, Roberts maintains, the Lord spoke to him (similar experiences are still reported by him from time to time): "Son, I am going to heal you, and you are to take my healing power to your generation." After Moncey said a healing prayer and put his hand on young Roberts, the transformation occurred thus: "Something struck my lungs and I began tingling throughout my entire body. A beautiful light engulfed me, and the next thing I knew, I was running back and forth on the big platform with my hands upraised, shouting at the top of my voice, 'I'm healed! I'm healed! I'm healed!' "

Two months later Oral Roberts began preaching, and for some twelve years conducted revivals in the South, intermittently serving as the pastor of small Pentecostal Holiness churches. During these years he also studied from time to time at both Oklahoma Baptist University and Phillips University, in Oklahoma. However, there was as yet nothing significant about his ministry, he was just one among hundreds of vagabond evangelists who traveled from small rural communities to low-income sections of Southern cities in their rattletrap automobiles, often with their families tagging along.

The reversal in Roberts' fortune came, according to his own account, when he began walking in his sleep and having trances. He reported that God again spoke to him, but only in general terms, telling him to take the healing power to the people. In order to get his specific instructions he subjected himself to fasting. After losing thirty-two pounds, writes Hayes B. Jacobs in his article "High Priest of Faith Healing" in *Harper's Magazine*, Roberts got his sign. He lay down on the floor to "have it out with God," determined never to rise until God had spoken to him. Then it happened. "Get on your feet," said God. "Go get in your car. Drive one block and turn right." After Roberts had followed these directions, God then said, "From this hour you will heal the sick and cast out devils by my power."

Roberts said he felt that the flames within were leaping out. He hurried home and told his wife Evelyn that he was breaking his fast, to cook him a meal, that the Lord had spoken to him. In the next service he held, Roberts states: "I laid my hand upon an old German woman who had been afflicted with a stiff hand for thirty-eight years. Suddenly she screamed at the top of her voice and shouted that she was healed." It was then, he says, that "I felt the whole world was waiting for me. I could go out with God's anointing and set the world on fire." [3]

As the story continues, he resigned his pastorate at Enid, Oklahoma, and moved to Tulsa, where he took over a healing series being conducted by a Brother Steve Pringle. For nine weeks the crowds came, partly as a result of reports of the healing of a blind man during the second week.[4] Roberts was always frank in explaining his healing "miracles," admitting that unless he felt the power of God surging through his right hand he would be unable to bring about any cures. "God heals; I don't," he explains.

Within two months Oral Roberts was on the way toward becoming one of America's most publicized evangelists. In 1948 he established Healing Waters, Inc., a "nonprofit, religious corporation," which later became the Oral Roberts Evangelistic Association, Inc., a multimillion dollar operation housed in three buildings, the largest being the seven-story Abundant Life Building, which at the time of its completion in 1957 was one of

Tulsa's architectural showpieces. By 1962 Roberts had in excess of 400 persons on his payroll and an annual budget of more than $4,000,000, which he met in a variety of ways—through special gifts from wealthy interests, pledges, or the "Blessing Pact," regular offerings (one night out of ten, Roberts retained for himself the contributions, or "love offerings," as he called them), royalties on books and recordings, revenue from the monthly publication, *Abundant Life*, with a circulation of 1,000,000, and the sale of souvenirs—"Jesus Heals" pins, "offering bags," and "anointed cloths." There are also investments in business, real estate, ranching, and educational institutions.

Oral Roberts crusades have covered the United States many times and have held meetings in Australia, Formosa, Japan, Poland, Finland, Puerto Rico, Canada, South Africa, and visited in Moscow.[5] At one point eight truck-trailers were required to move the Oral Roberts healing campaign equipment, worth $350,000, including tents with a capacity of 20,000, an aluminum platform for sixty people, and a 200,000-watt lighting and public address system.[6] The Crusade also owned two airplanes—a 12-passenger Aero Commander and a 4-passenger Bonanza for the use of the crusade team— and a fleet of automobiles. As a rule, the crowds taxed the available facilities. In 1955, Oral Roberts made his first television films and within a year he was a star performer, being heard on 600 radio stations and seen on 167 television stations weekly. His sermons were carried to more than a dozen foreign countries by short-wave broadcasts.[7]

Oral Roberts had the reputation of being the most sensational and spectacular evangelist in America. He had his own style and, realizing that he would be compared to Billy Graham, he made a statement for the record: "We're not in the same field. Graham is pricking the conscience of mankind with his hell fire and' brimstone. I think he's doing a good job. But I'm in another realm, emphasizing the love and goodness of God." [8] Roberts once referred to himself as a maverick, a "rebel against convention."

Describing his method, the evangelist said that before an evening service he spends about three hours alone in his hotel room outlining his sermon in detail. He does his writing on a lapboard with a loud-ticking clock before him, a sort of metronome to get his body and emotions synchronized. Roberts explained:

> "Its ticking seems to keep time as a spiritual transformation occurs. I become anointed with God's word and the spirit of the Lord builds up in me like a coiled spring. By the time I'm ready to go on, my mind is razor-sharp. I know exactly what I'm going to say and I'm feeling like a lion." [9]

Roberts, a student of practical psychology, never made his appearance in a revival service until he sensed that the audience was ready emotionally. He remained out of sight, letting the Rev. Robert DeWeese begin the meeting and lead the hymns, and then like the star of the show suddenly, at the right moment, frequently in a blue suit, bursts through a door behind the aluminum platform. Like the old-time evangelists, he too can play upon human emotions. He also has his routine, Bible in hand and the organ playing the theme song "Where the Healing Waters Flow."

Roberts became the song leader as he paced briskly across the platform. He might grab the microphone "by the throat, as if it were a demon." [10] To create a friendly atmosphere he would ask each person to shake hands with three people. To break down barriers he would add, "Some of you hifalutin' society folks loosen up and clap your hands." [11] Then to get more audience participation when the hymn was concluded, he asked, "Do you love the Lord tonight?" With one voice the con-

gregation answered with a resounding "Amen!" Then
he asked, "Do you love him with all your heart?" Then
there followed a louder "Amen!" Roberts proceeded to
exclaim, "Put up your hands and tell Him how much
you love Him!" Of course every hand was raised. He
shouted for the people to hold their hands higher so the
Lord could see their love. By this time the emotions
were running rather high.

So Roberts announced his text and went through it
three times, asking the audience to repeat it. For example, one night his text was "If God be for us, who can
be against us? " Then came a characterization of the
devil, "a roaring lion," and of sin, disease, demons, and
fear, "the offspring of the devil." At the core of his utterances against sin were the following: "There was a
time when there wasn't enough money on earth to give
to a Christian to lure him to smoke, to curse, or to drink!
If you really love God you don't need those things." [12]
One observer wrote of Roberts' style:

> While he delivers a supercharged message that may last
> two hours, he is a man possessed. He plays his congrega-
> tion like a symphony conductor. His voice crackles and
> blasts. His eyes flash and his expressive hands punctuate
> the words that rush from him in a torrent.[13]

In every detail the Roberts of the 1950's and 1960's
was a showman, never turning his back on a live television camera. When he made his altar call he asked the
people at home to raise their hands if they wanted his
prayers. Then they were asked to kneel beside their
radio or television sets, placing their hands on them to
keep the channels of the healing waters flowing either
to save the soul or, as he explained later in another part
of the service, to heal the body.

While the electronic organ played on, the people
filed toward the platform, many weeping, and Brothers
Hart Armstrong and Bob DeWeese directed them to an

adjoining tent to be enrolled so that their names could be forwarded to the church of their choice. Sometimes several thousand were supposedly "saved" at a single meeting; Roberts tried to average a million a year.

Then Oral Roberts disappeared temporarily from the big tent into another, referred to as the "invalid tent." Here awaited hundreds suffering from almost every disease or ailment known to medical science—terminal cancer cases, paralytics, schizophrenics, the blind, the deaf, arthritics, the lame, the palsied, the spastics— some escorted by friends or parents. Those admitted to the "healing line" had applied for and received a numbered card at an afternoon "faith building" service under the supervision of DeWeese, the campaign manager. On the card each person stated his ailment and authorized Roberts

> to use my name, picture, and statements made or testi-monials given by me in any public manner which you see fit. This includes, but is not limited to, television and radio programs, films and recordings, magazine articles, tracts, and books.[14]

A photographer was constantly on the move taking pictures for documentary evidence in publications. There was also printed on the card the warning:

> You will understand that Brother Roberts will not be able to minister to all during the same service, since hundreds are present to be healed. . . . But Brother Roberts will do his best to pray for you before the campaign is over. He reserves the right to pray for those who have special faith at any time during the meeting. Further, this card does not guarantee healing, since those coming for healing should come with a living, acting faith.[15]

The television cameras captured every movement as each fragment of this distressed and broken humanity went up a ramp in front of the crowd. Roberts' every gesture was also recorded as he slammed his hands on

foreheads and faces, shouting and screaming his magic
word "Heal!" [16] He explained that the laying on of
hands gently as in New Testament times would not
produce the psychological shock and mass suggestion.
Many ailments, he recognized, were psychosomatic in
origin. He was always the aggressor, pressing the individual with the question "Do you feel better?" The
twenty-two-year-old invalid wife of an Air Force
sergeant at Wichita Falls, Texas, wrote that she was
healed of injuries and illness that had confined her to a
wheelchair. She explained that she was watching a
Roberts service on television.[17] A lady in Springfield,
Massachusetts, reported that while listening to a healing prayer on the radio she was cured of multiple scle-
rosis that had left her paralyzed and blind.[18] Since estimates of numbers in the listening and viewing
audience reached sometimes into the millions for a single service, the volume of correspondence received
was monumental, providing endless examples of healing
for his publications.

Although critics of these faith-healing performances
(the Church of Christ being the most persistent) have
deplored the absence of medical verification, Roberts'
editors refer to the case histories and success reported
in the Roberts publications. The most frequent are
those instances where the subjects suffered from nervous depression, cancer, blindness, deafness, polio,
broken bones, tuberculosis, alcoholism, drug addiction,
and sugar diabetes.

Among the most interesting cures reported, one concerns a plumber and another, a businessman. The first
developed a "soft lump" on his right elbow while serving as a Seabee in the Navy. "There was absolutely
nothing to be done about it by the Navy doctors." He
explained that "Brother Roberts prayed a very simple
prayer while he laid his right hand on my elbow. Then
he turned to me and said, 'Forget about this lump in

Jesus' name.' I forgot about it for three days. . . . The lump was gone." The second case involved an elderly businessman in New York City who had a condition diagnosed as cancer of the colon. Upon the insistence of his wife the man attended a Roberts meeting and got a card to admit him to the "invalid tent." He testifies: "Brother Roberts laid his hand on my head and commanded the cancer to go. I felt no electrifying force, like some do. Instead, a peace flowed into my heart. . . . I was well." Believing that Roberts had cured him and not a physician, the businessman refused to return to the doctors for periodic checkups.[19]

As did the circuit riders and itinerant preachers of early times, Roberts offers a salvation removed from a social ethic and puritan in its morality. Tobacco, cosmetics, alcohol, movies, and the like are taboo. Perhaps unlike the older religiousness, a new idea was added— that Christianity involved more than the salvation of the soul; it involved the healing of both body and emotions.

Some predicted that Oral Roberts' decision to shift to the Methodist ministry could mark a change in his emphasis and style, but he views the change from Pentecostal to Methodist as a return to an earlier affiliation. For the past quarter of a century Methodism, even in rural America, has been moving away from the kind of emotionalism that characterized it in earlier times. Some of the minor sects such as the Pentecostals, Holiness groups, and Nazarenes have moved to fill a void left by groups that appealed to certain economic, social, and cultural levels. As to this change that has come over the Methodist church, a person by the name of Claudine, an admirer of the late faith healer A. A. Allen, reports: "I 'member back when I us in the Methodist Church. Lord, Mama usta shout her hair pins out and carry on, you know. But formality has come into the Church—an' Pride." [20]

Until his death on June 11, 1970, at age fifty-nine, Asa

Alonso Allen had also been in the forefront of the faith healers, and, like Roberts, had become a legend in his own lifetime. Allen was born in Arkansas. About thirty years ago he recognized the social change taking place in Methodism and switched to Pentecostalism. Though Allen's headquarters were at Miracle Valley, Arizona, on several thousand acres of desert terrain where he erected a religious community and college for training ministers of his persuasion, his formative years were spent in the South and Southwest. After thirty-four years in the ministry he had millions of followers of most racial groups who liked his brand of fundamentalism.

A. A. Allen Revivals, Inc., had become a big business with a solid financial base. In 1968 the gross income, exclusive of salaries for Allen and his two associate preachers, was $2,692,342. *Miracle Magazine,* with a monthly circulation of 350,000, was abundant in its coverage of the entire revivalistic enterprise. The headquarters building housed more than 175 employees who, with the latest office equipment and printing facilities, were involved in the processing of more than 55 million pieces of mail each year. Radio technicians were kept busy preparing Allen's daily broadcasts over a network of 58 stations. A large staff of television personnel prepared weekly programs for 43 stations. Allen also had a recording company to process the numerous albums of sermons and special gospel music.[21] He even had his own airstrip and plane. Twice a year he held a 17-day camp meeting, reminiscent of the antebellum religious festivals; thousands came from all over the country by automobile and all public means of transportation.

The meetings conducted by Allen bore a striking resemblance to those recorded by Peter Cartwright, John Lyle, Lorenzo Dow, and the many others celebrated in these pages. However, instead of the outdoor scene or tabernacle in an open rural setting, there was a coliseum at Miracle Valley. The drab homespun of the circuit rider had given way to an iridescent lavender suit or pink coat with blue trousers to create a better image over color television. A shaggy horse laden with saddlebags and blankets had surrendered to a caravan of five "A. A. Allen Revivals" vans and house trailers. The star of the show with his entourage traveled in a private plane or new Lincoln Continental, having been preceded by a corps of advance men. Except for such recent innovations as organ, drums, and piano combo, the rest seemed about the same, that is, the gospel songs, the message, and human behavior. These never change. In the words of the song "The Old-Time Religion": "It was good for Paul and Silas; and it's good enough for me." Whether at Cane Ridge or Miracle Valley, yesterday or today, the old-time religion seems to make men shake, dance, weep, fall prostrate, shout, speak in tongues, or make a joyful noise.

Allen made a special plea for members of his radio and television audiences to send him their most important or urgent prayer requests so that he might ask his entire camp-meeting congregation to share in the praying. He asked the distressed individual to send an apron or a handkerchief to be prayed over according to Acts 19:11–12 and to enclose a self-addressed, stamped envelope so that the item might be returned when it had been prayed over or had hands laid upon it and it had been blessed.

Since the early camp meetings, a striking change has occurred in the types of people who attend. Timothy Flint in his *History of the Western States* observed that in the early days a good cross section of society was in attendance. William Hedgepeth, a senior editor for *Look,* in 1969 at A. A. Allen's meeting in the Georgia Livestock Exhibition Building in Atlanta observed a group that might lead one to believe he was in the reception room of a charity hospital in a large city. The people, he wrote, seemed to

> cling shyly together like dazed survivors of some gigantic shipwreck. Here they gathered with their vague uneasiness and private eagerness to be thrust somehow into the grips of something overwhelming: sodden-eyed parents with drowsy children; jut-jawed old black men; bearded women; dwarfs; blind ladies; men with giant goiters; lay preachers; lunatics; splayed feet; faded eyes; tight skirts and teased-up hair; varicose veins; hook hands; work shirts; calico and, here and there, a wan, brief smile like a piece of cracked pottery. They are a cacophony of smells and a scramble of ages and shapes and races and bottomless frustrations—each sharing some hue of vague unlabeled loneliness and a need for some faint coloration to the grayness of their days. They come in quest of soothing balm, or at least a seizure. They are enamored of ambiguity, fascinated by paradox: oh, just to see a glimmer of a genuine demon, to feel his eerie, scaly tail; to lose control, to scream and spit and to be a part of a larger something that is simple and vastly incomprehensible. God is, at once, their anguish and their consolation.[22]

Allen noted certain characteristics and trends within his segment of evangelical Christianity, "The real move to God today is among the colored people." He explained: "The Scripture says the common people receive Him [Jesus] gladly. But the religious leaders were the ones who killed Him. The colored people right now are the common people." Welcoming a wave of anti-intellectualism, he added: "The revival isn't breaking out among intellectuals. The Bible says much learning hath made thee mad. So we're making no special effort to reach intellectuals. Jesus didn't." [23]

Allen was something of a seer when he predicted a trend in his type of emotional Christianity. He saw a greater popularity of his kind of fundamentalism and spontaneous religious expression resulting from a discontent with the "cold, dead hand of denominationalism." He believed God was "opening the eyes of the people. Most people realize that the church is nothing but a social-welfare agency." Recognizing his unique position in the forefront of his type of revivalism, he said:

> "There's no evangelists left that offer us any competition. We've got the field. Back in the late '40's and '50's, Jack Coe, Oral Roberts, O. L. Jaggers and 200 others, you know, there were 200 evangelists all praying for the sick, having healing revivals. Now they're nonexistent." [24]

The faith-healing episodes in A. A. Allen's meetings, like those of Oral Roberts, attracted regional attention when they were in progress; however, neither really wanted to be designated as faith healers per se. They considered themselves to be gospel missionaries and believed that God did the healing. The case histories do reflect certain strange behaviors, as did those in the meetings of old. On the copyright page of *Miracle Magazine* appears the rationale:

> This is a religious publication published for the purpose of glorifying God as Savior of the whole man, body, soul, and spirit. Accounts of healing, deliverance and miracles, as printed in *Miracle Magazine* are testimonies of those who report to have experienced the same. Detailed attention has been given in reporting and editing these testimonials to avoid distortion and exaggeration of the original personal or written declarations. Utmost care has been taken to assure the accuracy of all testimonies before publication and A. A. Allen Revivals, Inc. and *Miracle Magazine* assume no responsibility for the veracity of any such report, nor do they accept responsibility as to the degree of permanency of reported healings, deliverances or miracles since the Bible itself declares that for those who do not continue to live for God, even worse things may come (John 5:14).

The issues of *Miracle Magazine* report miraculous episodes and strange phenomena from all sections of
America, similar both in motivation and responses to
the religious "exercises" of the early nineteenth century. Then there was no scientific or psychological
idiom the pulpit could use to describe a personal religious experience as psychotherapy or to recognize its
therapeutic value. Salvation was identified primarily
with soul and a future life; today it concerns also the
health of body, mind, and spirit.

However, the following episodes from experiences of
people in the Southwest, reported by *Miracle Magazine*, do reflect certain similarities to the early phenomena.[25]

A Fort Worth, Texas, woman wrote:

> On May 12, 1968, my daughter was hit by a car about
> 6:30 P.M. We didn't know how bad she was for a while.
> She was knocked 35 to 40 feet down the street. My
> sister-in-law called Miracle Valley and asked for prayer.
> My daughter and I went to the hospital and the doctors
> were amazed! Ruthie only had a broken left upper arm,
> and bruises. All kinds of X-rays were made and there was
> nothing else wrong.
>
> She was sent home the same night; and now, one
> would not think there was ever anything wrong. She is
> playing like always.
>
> All of the time she was hurt, Ruthie kept telling the
> doctors that God was in her heart, and He would help.
> We know it was only God's answer to prayer that she was
> not hurt worse or killed. We thank God that there is a
> place to call when something is wrong! Ruthie is just
> doing wonderfully now! [26]

A Westel, Tennessee, man explained that through the
television ministry he was delivered from tobacco:

> One Sunday morning I was looking at Bro. Allen's televi-
> sion broadcast. He prayed for a man who said he was
> choking to death. When he prayed, the man commenced

speaking in tongues. He received the Baptism in the Holy Ghost! The Spirit moved on me, and I cried for a solid week. I laid my cigarettes down after smoking about fifty years. I haven't touched any to this day; that's been better than seven years now. God baptized me with the Holy Ghost, sanctified me, and set me upon my feet! [27]

A woman from Macon, Georgia, submitted the following testimony:

Thank God for sending you [Allen] to Macon. For three years I had been propped up on five pillows to be able to sleep. I couldn't lie down. I had a tumor. The doctor said that where it was, I had a fifty-fifty chance. So I had to live with it. I went to the meeting Wednesday night and went through the prayer line. You just touched me, and I was healed. Now I just sleep on one pillow and don't take any medicine.[28]

An evangelist (Tony Barnes) reported on the Miracle Revival Campaign in Atlanta, Georgia:

From the platform I noticed three people in wheelchairs sat on the front row. One hadn't walked in five years; one hadn't walked in two years; the other was not only crippled, but blind also. The music and fervent singing filled the tent; the atmosphere was charged with the power of God. People stood to clap their hands and to shout and praise God. My cup was filled as I listened to the choir sing, but it ran over when suddenly the lady who had not walked in five years came out of her wheelchair and began walking!

I watched the third man work with his legs, but he stayed in the chair. I closed my eyes and began to sing with the choir. Suddenly, I heard a new shout from the congregation! There, walking around, was the third man! Not only was he walking, but also seeing! Then, all over the tent, people were being healed! [29]

The evangelist went on to explain that no human hand had touched these afflicted individuals. God had touched them, he affirmed, with healing through the "lively revival music." This was a special anointing from God and the results could not have come about from just anyone's playing and singing.

The author of this book recalls a similar occurrence in the late 1940's in a large white camp meeting at Bessemer, Alabama, and another in Birmingham a few blocks from his apartment. Following a "devil-chasing" sermon and spirited singing accompanied by tambourines, shouting, and "speaking in unknown tongues," an epidemic of the "jumps" broke out: young and old, the lame and palsied, cast aside their crutches and canes and began jumping into the air with violent screams and shouts. Whether their cures were permanent he has no way of knowing, but they certainly had no symptoms of their afflictions when the bedlam started. It was a recurrence of the nineteenth-century religious "exercises." In another meeting, this time near Tuscaloosa, Alabama, on the banks of the Black Warrior river, the minister painted such an attractive picture of heaven and God's omnipresence that many people ran out of the church, began climbing up the walls and into the surrounding trees, reaching upward as if trying to touch God.

Again in *Miracle Magazine,* a man from Ashland, Kentucky, wrote about his healing experience:

> I was reading one of Bro. Allen's magazines one evening when I saw the words, "Dial a Miracle." The doctors were going to amputate one of my legs, and eventually the other one, because of a clogged artery. I dialed a miracle! In ten minutes' time, God had moved the obstruction.
>
> Later, when the technician gave me a blood test, I told her about it. She said, "Well, that has never happened before. It's not possible in medical science for a dead pulse in a limb to ever come back." When the doctor checked, he said my pulse was there. Thank God, I've still got my legs! [30]

From El Campo, Texas, a young woman wrote:

On January 18, 1968, the doctor told me that the baby I
was carrying was dead, and that at the end of the week
he was going to put me in the hospital for surgery.
   I made a phone call to Miracle Valley the next night,
and for the first time I began to feel life. I told my doctor
the miracle God had done for me. My baby, who was
supposed to have been dead, was born in the very best of
health. I call him my miracle baby! Thanks to God and to
our praying friends who had faith for a miracle! [31]

One instance of healing was indeed a puzzle to the
closest friends of a New Orleans woman who sent her
testimony to the *Miracle Magazine:*

I had curvature of the spine and couldn't walk.
   While listening to Bro. Allen's program one morning,
he said to lay hands upon the radio as a point of contact,
and we would be healed. I laid my hand upon the radio
and felt the power of God come through! I believed God,
and He healed me! [32]

Just as miraculous was the experience of a Pensacola,
Florida, woman who testified that

God healed me of a cancerous condition in the Birmingham, Alabama, Campaign in 1959. I was healed
while sitting in my seat. The doctors had told my
daughter-in-law I wouldn't live a year.[33]

A most recent manifestation of healing finds expression in the 700 Club Telethon, based in the South but
national in scope. During the second weekend of April
1973, the Club held one of its telethons in Houston,
Texas. The ultimate objective of the enterprise was to
raise funds to keep this particular style of religious
broadcast on the air for a minimum of twenty-five hours
a week over a network of stations. The facilities of
Channel 26 in Houston were used for the forty-eight-
hour program. A master of ceremonies opened with a
protracted prayer for those in the Gulf Coast area with

afflictions (physical, emotional, and spiritual); then the fifty telephone assistants received calls from those who reported healing results. These transcriptions were carried by pages to ministers at the microphone who relayed the message, exhorting in a fundamentalist style. After hours of testimonials the telethon turned to the more mundane matter of fund-raising. Pledges were called in and recorded on the giant board in the style of an election night report. Random excerpts from the testimonials were read with editorial comments by the minister in charge.

A boy reported that he had suffered from a rash for more than a month, but as a result of the ministers' and the people's prayers it went away.

The exhorter said he was "listening to the voice of the Lord but with all the telephoning and great commotion of the great things happening it is hard to hear Him."

A woman was having trouble from nearsightedness and could hardly see her television set; "she prayed, the Lord touched her," and she was healed.

A woman stated that she was cured of her "miscarrying womb."

A man had a knot behind the ear, another had a growth on the back of the leg, still another had suffered for two years with a knot on the neck. They were healed.

"The Lord knows who you are and where you are."

Other instances of healing were reported: infection in the sex organs and bladder cured, a heart murmur cured (the individual gave his address), a kidney problem gone, cataracts removed.

"God has been doing a lot of things with eyes. This is like the man who was blind and came to Jesus and said, 'Now I can see.' Jesus is alive. We have a great God. He lives. He is risen. Praise God. Praise the Lord."

A man who had a pain in his back for two years and

could not bend over testified that he could now bend over completely.

A person who was about to commit suicide sought the advice of a friend and the Lord cured her of the depression.

A sprained foot and a torn muscle were cured when surgery had failed. "Where was the torn muscle; in the back of the left leg? Yes, that was the one the Lord was talking about."

A broken pelvis was giving terrible pain. It was cured.

"This gets gooder and gooder. If it gets better we are going to take off and fly or something."

Several hernia patients were cured. The minister identified each as the one he was praying for by the location of the injury.

A woman had come with eyes crossed, but only one eye was corrected at first. The woman was asked to put her hand on the other eye while they prayed together. Everyone was asked to pray. However, one eye was "still blurry."

An asthma attack was checked. The doctor telephoned that the patient was all right.

"The telephone lines are full with the people calling in. The power of God is moving in Houston, Texas. Jesus said He would do it."

A leukemia case was cured. Another cataract was removed.

"Miracles! If you could understand everything about God, then He is not God. God is God. He works as God, does as He pleases. If you believe that one day God can take a pile of bones and resurrect them into a new shape, surely you can believe He can take a cataract off an eye, cure a lame leg. I believe in the resurrection of the body. Can't you believe in the healing of the body? He's healing people in Texas. He's saving people in Texas."

"Ulcers, diabetes, infection of the ear, lump under the arm, cancer, tumor, broken leg, broken nose, voice gone, one handicapped from birth, warts on the hands—all cured."

"The thing we don't want to happen is for all this to stop. Nothing can stop this. Some time during the week-end we've got to raise the money to keep this program on the air. We must stay on the air until Jesus comes. Pray a fund-raising telethon! "

And with this note the direction of the program began to change from healing to the solicitation of pledges.

We observed in the old camp meetings that sometimes even children would become affected and feel so strongly the urge to preach that they might climb up on a stump or wagon to speak. During the last twenty-five years several children have performed such remarkable feats that they received unusual attention in the press. For example, the child evangelist Renee Martz had already converted thousands by the age of eight. In more than a year she spoke to audiences totaling two hundred thousand in almost every major city in the world. According to her father, Jack Martz, Renee had "led six thousand souls up to the altar to confess their sins and accept Jesus Christ." This slender, brown-haired, brown-eyed child, who wore cowgirl boots in revival meetings and preached with fervor and conviction, made an international reputation. Like the children of old she "felt the call." She said, "I heard a voice somewhere, 'You go and preach the gospel.' " [34] Also in the manner of the older crusaders, she cried out against amusement centers, particularly the movies.

Among the most celebrated and controversial of these child evangelists was Marjoe Gortner. When he was three years of age his parents, who were evangelists, began programming his thoughts and gestures until by the age of six he was a religious automaton or puppet resembling a performer in the old medicine shows and vaudevilles. His Bible readings, sermons, and rituals were all memorized. His mother, referred to in his biography, *Marjoe, a Modern Miracle,* as Sister Marge, manipulated his performance, sitting behind him in the pulpit, by the use of certain cue words—"Hallelujah," to accelerate; "Glory," to slow down; "Praise God" or "Thank you, Jesus," to take the offering.[35] Marjoe learned early that one of the fringe benefits of saving souls was filling the collection buckets with bills. He estimated that by the time he was twelve he had shared in collecting $3,000,000.

Marjoe abandoned the sawdust trail when he reached maturity. He became a hippie. He attempted to organize a rock group, becoming a devotee of Bob Dylan and expounding social justice.[36] Then he retraced the itinerary of his childhood and discovered that the people he had hoped to help transform had remained untouched by the present world. "I remember," he says, "all the crazy hangups they had about the things like movies and short skirts or anything else they could think of to label sin. But now I really felt I had something I believed in which I wanted to say to them." [37] Then he threw himself into the evangelical circuit again, but this time with a social gospel, which did not take hold. His failure drove him to a cynical belief that the Pentecostal people demanded the bizarre and the sensuous, so he resumed the former motif of hellfire and damnation, with some degree of success. But basically he disliked both himself and the people who crowded to hear his exhortations. Yet he gave them the kind of gospel they demanded.

The next step in his career was the movie *Marjoe,* which was billed as a razzle-dazzle nonfiction feature. It is a sort of 1972 edition of Sinclair Lewis' *Elmer Gantry* in which he gives a behind-the-scenes confession to his five-man camera crew before each filming of a live revival meeting. He poses as a typical evangelist, demonstrating, to the horror and dismay of many establishment evangelicals, the "tricks of the trade," some of which were actually practiced in frontier Christianity. The most controversial portions of the film were those dealing with "a swinging black revival meeting in Detroit," "a Pentecostal preacher coolly discussing the land he had bought in Brazil," and "another shouting from the pulpit that the Cadillac he drives is God's own gift." [38] Also much to the chagrin of many participating in both nineteenth-century spectacles and today's versions is the suggestion that some of the spiritual ecstasy was a sexual response.

Marjoe admits that he deliberately burned his bridges behind him, but he considered the movie experience worth it all. Even though he proved himself something of a "quack," he also exposed the "quackery" in so much of the religious emotionalism. The movie undoubtedly has cast a bad light upon other evangelists. Brian Rudd, revival preacher, said, "He's like a banker who embezzles money trying to get all other bankers to look like crooks." [39]

Interviewed with others on the NBC television *Today* show, Billy Graham stated that the *Marjoe* film was a complete "distortion" of the type of evangelism that had gone on in his meetings. He made specific reference to the pressure on the congregations during the taking of collections. Graham also saw the film as "a deliberate attack against the new religious awakening that is sweeping primarily among young people in the United States today both in the Catholic Church and the Protestant Church and in the Jewish Synagogue." He added, "We have probably, in my judgment, the greatest religious awakening among youth today in history, and they had this great Explo '72 down in Dallas, where they had a hundred thousand young people, and this film was released immediately after that and it seems to me that somewhere back of that [i.e., the release of the film] there was something deliberate." Graham concluded that he believed Marjoe had been manipulated, first by his parents and then by film makers. While Graham admitted that Marjoe's type of evangelism may have existed back in the frontier days, particularly in the South, he could not believe it was prevalent at the present time.

Explo '72, to which Billy Graham refers, was a week-long rally in June 1972, in the Cotton Bowl. A crowd of 80,000 young people from the United States and from seventy-five foreign countries gathered to shout, sing, pray, and praise Jesus. This mammoth meeting was sponsored by Campus Crusade for Christ International, an evangelical group with the goal "to take the message of Jesus to every individual in America by 1976 and the whole world by 1980." [40]

Seventy thousand lighted candles at the service on the last night in the Cotton Bowl may have suggested the Cane Ridge meetings where the pine knots glowed in the wooded groves. The religious week ended with a nine-hour rock festival in which 150,000 young people participated on a freeway site in downtown Dallas. Johnny Cash, the singer of country and western music, led the performance, and he reflected the spirit of the occasion with the comment, "I have tried drugs and a little of everything else and there is nothing in the world more soul-satisfying than having the kingdom of God building inside you and growing." [41]

Most of the Jesus People who are rebelling against middle-class culture find that "acceptance of Jesus Christ as Savior has given them a whole new purpose in life." [42] They are reviving a type of traditional fundamentalism that was prevalent during the early nineteenth century, with a belief in heaven and hell and a literal interpretation of the Bible. Like the nineteenth-century groups, they react against churches that do not have their enthusiasm for the gospel. Also they resemble their revivalist ancestors in their crusade against drinking and smoking, and (today) drugs. Like their forebears in the South, who endorsed the "peculiar institution" of slavery, they too are against social action and argue that the best way to change society is to change the individual. They proclaim, as the frontier preachers proclaimed, "Ye must be born again." Their appeal is essentially to the emotions and against formal theology.

The more extreme of the Jesus People are referred to as Jesus Freaks. In 1971 one such group had six outposts, including a colony of four hundred at Thurber, Texas, where it conducts the "Texas Soul Clinic." The group had a growth rate of one per day, recruitment efforts generally using entertainment—i.e., spirited music, sometimes a type of rock music. This group is especially interested in helping those whose lives have been blighted by crime, drugs, and venereal diseases. No drugs are allowed. "The highest I have ever been is with Jesus" is a comment frequently heard. With no faith in today's values, the idea of working for money is rejected. Six hours a day of Bible-reading is expected of everyone. The group's prime targets are the revolutionaries—militants who would burn down and use force. "Jesus laid down a spiritual revolution," they maintain. With "the baptism in the name of Jesus Lord" they receive the Holy Ghost and learn to speak in tongues. As in the nineteenth century, there are repeated predictions of the end of the world. In many details the Jesus movement offers a new twist to the older religiousness and a clear indication that emotional Christianity is not on the decline.

Those who argue that emotional religion has almost vanished from the Southern scene have only to turn on their radios after eleven thirty P.M. For thirty-five years the author of these pages has listened to these programs—in Arkansas, Tennessee, Alabama, and Texas. He has been particularly fascinated by the way the sermons build up to a climax, at which point the exhorter begins the "holy whine" just as did his earlier counterparts. One experience in Birmingham left an indelible impression. An Assemblies of God minister was broadcasting, all alone, in a small, soundproof room of dimensions about 7 by 8 feet, with only a tiny glass plate in the door through which radio personnel could make periodic examinations of the activities inside. There he was, clutching the microphone by the throat from time to time, waving his arms frantically, jumping up and down, shouting his lungs out, almost bouncing off the walls, as he worked himself into a frenzy. Although this was almost three decades ago, it was the pulpit style used by Marjoe Gortner in his movie interpretation.

William C. Martin has written with scholarly perception of this "great church of the airways." He is concerned with preachers like Brother Al ("that's A. L. Brother Al"); the Reverend Frederick J. Eikerenkoetter II ("Reverend Ike"); C. W. Burpo ("Spelled 'B' as in Bible"); Kathryn Kuhlman ("Have . . . you . . . been . . . waiting . . . for . . . me? "); A. A. Allen, who has already been discussed in some detail; and Garner Ted Armstrong, who speaks through a magazine, *Plain Truth*, and a television show, *The World Tomorrow*. There are also J. Charles Jessup of Gulf Port, Mississippi; Bill Beeny of St. Louis, Missouri; Glenn Thompson of Paragould, Arkansas; James Bishop Carr of Palmdale, California; David Terrell, and Billy Walker.[43]

Garner Ted Armstrong, as spokesman for Ambassador College, attempts to instruct on topics such as narcotics, crime, pollution, and heresies with reference to the Bible for the whole truth about the present and future. Conservative C. W. Burpo speaks for God, Nixon, and constitutional government but against sex education. The popular radio gospel preachers are those who offer solutions to everyday problems—financial, physical, emotional, and spiritual. These are referred to as the "healers and blessers." [44] Like the faith healers we have already observed, they cited phenomenal successes. Like members of the medical profession, certain of the radio healers specialize. For example, Brother Al would appear to be a foot specialist: "God can take corns, bunions, and tired feet, and massage them with his holy love and make them well." [45]

Radio evangelists defray the cost of their programs by requesting contributions. Brother Al makes his appeal to the faithful to send "God's perfect offering—$7.00, not $6.00; not $8.00, but $7.00. A better gift would be $77, God's two perfect numbers, although any multiple of seven is meritorious." Then he adds, "God told me to ask for this. You know I don't talk like this. It's got to be God. God told me he had a lot of bills to pay. Obey God—just put the cash inside the envelope." [46] Glenn Thompson also makes God a cosolicitor as he points out that most of the world's ills, ranging from crabgrass and garden bugs to Communism and the bomb, may be attributed to man's robbing God. He continues: "You've got God's money in your wallet. You old stingy Christian. No wonder we've got all these problems. You want to know how you can pay what you owe? God is speaking through me. God said, 'Inasmuch as you do it unto one of these, you do it unto me.' God said, 'Give all you have for the gospel's sake.' My address is Brother Glenn, Paragould, Arkansas." [47]

Perhaps the striking difference in motivation between the nineteenth-century revivalists and today's evangelists of the minor sects may be put in simple terms. Certainly the latter strive to populate heaven with derelicts, but they eloquently and passionately labor to fill the buckets and plastic wastebaskets with money. Peter Cartwright would regard all of this tribe as religious con men, but his era could not understand the temptations that arise in an affluent society.

Whether the religious extravaganza occurred in the eighteenth, the nineteenth, or the twentieth century, there is one striking truism. Groups of people are no more intelligent than the individuals who make up the units, but a crowd can be chaotic. Aldous Huxley, in a chapter entitled "Propaganda Under a Dictatorship" (in his *Brave New World Revisited*), suggests what seems to be in part a commentary on religious exercises and excessive emotionalism. Huxley writes:

> Assembled in a crowd, people lose their powers of reasoning and their capacity for moral choice. Their suggestibility is increased to the point where they cease to have any judgment or will of their own. They become very excitable, they lose all sense of individual or collective responsibility, they are subject to sudden accesses of rage, enthusiasm and panic. In a word, a man in a crowd behaves as though he had swallowed a large dose of some powerful intoxicant. He is a victim of what I have called "herd-poisoning." Like alcohol, herd-poison is an active, extraverted drug. The crowd-intoxicated individual escapes from responsibility, intelligence and morality into a kind of frantic animal mindlessness.[48]

The demagogue has studied the effects of herd-poisoning, and as an orator, knows how to appeal to the "hidden forces" that motivate behavior. The more eloquent "firebrands" of the Southern pulpit, likewise, knew how to address the masses of agrarian communicants, already primed with herd-poison. There is a similarity between the demagoguery of a dictator and the dogmatizing of a bigot. Both are committed to an ideological uniformity—political for the one and spiritual for the other—with assurances of reward for those who triumph or endure.

9
Emotionalism
in Education and Politics

THE TWENTIETH CENTURY, like the nineteenth, has
been subjected to controversy arising within the framework of the old-time faith. Protestant sects in the
South continue to keep a watchful eye upon educational institutions, never questioning their right to in-
tervene in the affairs of private or public concerns, if
any behavior or ideology of a questionable nature appears. As early as 1917, writes Kenneth K. Bailey in his
*Southern White Protestantism in the Twentieth Cen-
tury*, the Southern Baptist Education Commission expressed the aspirations of conservative elements when
it looked forward to the time when "only God-fearing
men and women may teach in our state schools, from
the common school to the university." [1] As late as 1959,
four members of the Texas Legislature approached the
problem more directly. They attempted to introduce a
bill that would require employees in state-supported
institutions to pledge belief in a Supreme Being; a mea-
sure, they confessed, designed to prevent the spread of
atheism. One of the Representatives, who had a list of
names of professors ready to be turned over to the
House Investigating Committee, said: "We have been
advised that some instructors . . . are not only athe-
ists but are expounding opinions in class not only
about atheism but derogatory about religion." Violation

of the proposed law would carry a $100 to $1000 fine.[2]

The twentieth century has brought little change in the churches' attitudes toward some of the so-called sins of the earlier period. The Southern Presbyterian General Assembly, notes Kenneth Bailey, ruled in 1893 that dancing was an offense punishable by excommunication. Gambling, attending the theater, card-playing, Sabbath-breaking, and drinking alcoholic beverages are some of the other vices that have bothered Southern orthodoxy, with Episcopalianism being among the exceptions.[3] As late as 1937, a Southern Baptist Convention meeting in Anniston, Alabama, adopted by strong vote a resolution expressing objection to the use of tobacco. It was the modern dance, however, that aroused the greatest concern in the 1920's. One Baptist minister reflects a common attitude when he complained that the "waltz, turkey trot, grizzly bear, bunny hug, buzzard lope and the shimmy, ad nauseam ad infinitum" took place not in "full evening dress" but in "full evening undress." He added that women often removed their corsets before dancing so that "sexual feelings may be more easily and intensely aroused." [4]

The pulpit also became alarmed over feminine fashions. One Baptist minister watched with fear the rising hemline of women's dresses. He observed, writes Bailey, that "scant dress is usually accompanied by scant morals" and that "if some of the dresses continue the same ratio for the next twenty-five years that they have maintained for the past ten years, they will be exactly fifteen feet above the head." [5] Of course, preachers had no such fears in the nineteenth century, but Methodists and Baptists called attention to the degrading effects of luxuries in the forms of frills, lace, and jewelry.

The anti-intellectualism of nineteenth-century evangelical Christianity has moderated somewhat, with certain exceptions. However, accepting doctrine as fact has made for inevitable conflict with new theories and ideas. The Bible Belt concept has served some as an insulation against the world of change. For instance, fundamentalists too frequently have attempted to build a wall around the public school system as a safeguard against the planting of doubts in children's minds. The old-time religion and the faith of their fathers had served for more than a century; it had become a sieve through which knowledge had to be transmitted.

Since the 1920's the conflict between fundamentalism and the theory of evolution has plagued public education. Mostly in the South the state legislatures have come to grips with Darwinian science. Kenneth Bailey quotes from Maynard Shipley's "Growth of the Anti-Evolution Movement," in *Current History and Forum* for May 1930, where it is shown that every Southern legislature, save Virginia's, deliberated and redeliberated the issue throughout the 1920's. A record of the activity is as follows: in North Carolina in 1925 and 1927; in South Carolina in 1922, 1927, and 1928; in Georgia in 1923 and 1925; in Florida in 1923, 1925, and 1927; in Alabama in 1923 and 1927; in Mississippi in 1926; in Louisiana in 1926; in Texas in 1923, 1925, and 1929; in Oklahoma in 1923 and 1927; in Arkansas in 1927; [6] in Tennessee in 1923 and 1925; and in Kentucky in 1922 and 1926.[7] Some bills included denunciation of Darwinism, exclusion of books containing evolution, withholding of funds from schools where the ideas existed, assessing of fines, and rebuke of the offenders. However, only in Oklahoma, Florida, Tennessee, Mississippi, and Arkansas did any of the measures get through both houses of the legislature.

In March 1925, the Tennessee legislature passed its bill forbidding in the public schools of the state the teaching of "any theory which denies the story of the Divine creation of man as taught in the Bible" and which teaches "instead that man is descended from a lower form of animals." A group of pranksters, bored with the quiet atmosphere in the town of Dayton, Tennessee—a typical Southern community—badgered John T. Scopes, a biology teacher, into changing his lesson plan to inject Darwin's theory of evolution into one of his lectures. "It was a hoax, a joke, to stir up some excitement," reported one of the students to the author of these pages. "Some of the fellows wanted to put a little life in the town, and we did."

Scopes was brought to trial on July 10, the prosecution being conducted by the attorney general of the state, who was assisted by the famed orator and three-time Democratic presidential candidate, William Jennings Bryan. The defense was headed by a master of cross-examination, Clarence S. Darrow, supported by Dudley F. Malone and Arthur G. Hayes.

On July 21, Scopes was found guilty of violating the state law and was fined $100. Bryan died of a heart attack five days later, after a humiliating ordeal, though he was technically victorious. Two years later the appellate court of Tennessee reviewed the case and reversed the verdict, preventing efforts to get the case before the United States Supreme Court.

Periodically one reads in the press of some teacher who has brought down the wrath of a patron by talking about evolution in the classroom. According to the *Birmingham News* (February 11, 1948), an English teacher and coach at a school in the Atlanta, Georgia, system was assailed by a local Baptist minister because he had "taught the story of creation of man contrary to the Bible's account." The minister attacked the teacher in a way that was characteristic: "There is no shred of proof to the theory of evolution." The teacher attempted to defend himself thus: "I always thought I was just a Christian. I'm teaching English and not making any attempt to teach biology or religion. During my early American literature class I said the language developed over a long period, that, like man, it didn't just happen, and that mankind started from lower forms and didn't reach the human stage overnight." This controversy was reminiscent of the Scopes incident.

In 1963, when two Memphis State University student teachers were rebuked by the high school principal for explaining the theory of evolution before a biology class, the 1925 law was again discussed but not challenged. Bailey reports Scopes's pessimism when he was asked by a reporter to comment on the new furor: "I think the case was lost in 1925. We fought a good battle but we didn't win very much. I would hope it would be different today, but I don't really know." [8]

In April 1967, the board of trustees of Jacksboro High School in Tennessee dismissed a science teacher for allegedly teaching evolution. The episode came only one day after the state house of representatives voted 58–27 to repeal the state's antievolution law; however, the state senate, after vigorous debate and national attention, did not concur in the house's action. There was a tied vote. The legislature agreed on an amendment that would ban the teaching of evolution as fact but would not ban the teaching of evolution as theory. The young man is reported as saying that he would drop the case if he were paid a year's salary. The National Education Association had offered aid in the suit against the school board, attacking the constitutionality of the law that had been violated. The East Tennessee Civil Liberties Union promised both legal and financial help. [9]

Legally, the Scopes trial and the two other instances in the same state should be considered a Tennessee problem, but the notoriety of the Scopes trial made it a Southern problem, partly as a result of editorializing by H. L. Mencken. He helped crystallize the identity of the problem and gave the whole sector its title of Bible Belt. The name has endured. Evangelical Christianity came to be considered as the unmistakable spring from which the corrupting influence flowed.

However, national rebuke merely solidified Southern faith in its righteousness and quickened its suspicion of and hostility toward outside influences that threatened its way of life. A school board or college governing board will not hesitate to terminate faculty members who seem to threaten this way of life, whether the issue is a difference of opinion on religion or on civil rights. Communism, atheism, agnosticism, socialism, federalism, and integration are some of the concepts bandied around when the inquisition is formulating its verdict. Politicians and some religionists have found in the "faith of our fathers" a unifying emotionalism for a strategy to preserve the *status quo* against alien beliefs.

Whether statesman or demagogue, he who would communicate successfully with Southern folk would do well to understand their culture and behavior, and above all their inflammable spirit. The political stump orators have understood the people's range. Between the times of Davy Crockett and Huey Long many figures have moved into state and national prominence by exploiting prejudice and the desire to believe. The John the Baptists of the older evangelical tradition had cried out in the wilderness to prepare the way for later spokesmen who transmitted the same faith. Political orators have studied their examples by imitating their intonation of voice, their earthy images of field and farm, and their deep convictions.

Governors like George C. Wallace of Alabama and Lester Maddox of Georgia have been aware of their forebears. They have also been aware of a prevailing unity housed in the emotions of the common folk. For example, on the night of his defeat by Attorney General John Patterson in the campaign of 1958 for governor, Wallace learned his lesson. He confessed that he had pursued a moderate, rational course on the race question, while Patterson had appealed to all the conservatives and reactionaries, including the Ku Klux Klan.

That night Wallace said: "I made a pledge. No one is ever going to out-nigger me again." No one has. Now he is a winner, so far as state politics is concerned. At the national level in the 1968 Presidential election his American Party was a powerful force in its appeal to conservative voters. Campaigning in 1972 for the Democratic nomination he was making great progress until he was struck down by an attempted assassination and was compelled to withdraw from active participation. However, he polarized the issues, and his absence from the ballot helped to elect Richard Nixon to a second term as President. He recognized the deep-seated unity that existed, which he related to a certain way of life. He volunteered to protect it from all outside influences—all the foreign isms that alarm the old-time believers and seem to threaten their way of life. Men like Wallace and Maddox understand these Southern religious folk and can predict mass reaction. They are realists in a strict and practical sense, because they equate religious solidarity and political solidarity.

The student of both Southern religion and politics has only to view the Presidential campaign of 1928 to see that the two may be inseparable. With prohibition and Al Smith's Catholicism as issues, Southern Baptist and Methodist denominations were instrumental in carrying a solidly Democratic South for Republican Herbert Hoover. Never before have preachers responded as individuals so vigorously and so effectively on a group basis to crystallize public opinion. Any friction that may have resulted from denominational differences was quickly arrested in a concerted effort to uphold prohibition and denounce Smith's Romanism. Invective became the order of the day. Kenneth Bailey records the ministerial tone in his comments on a speech of the Rev. J. W. Hunt, president of the Methodist McMurry College. Hunt charged that Smith would listen to foreign influences and turn the White House into a Catholic shrine. In another speech he exclaimed that the "chicken stealing, crap-shooting, bootlegging negro crowd" was supporting Smith, who was a "dirty, drunken bum." [10] The more radical religionists were identified with the Ku Klux Klan on the issues of Catholicism and race. The structure of the old-time religion, what Mencken labeled as Bible Belt attitudes, made this Southern unity possible.

Radical religionists have also been concerned with integration and the curriculum in the public schools. They have been hostile toward civil rights and toward change in most forms. They have been known to raise objection to textbook adoptions by citizens committees and legislative committees.

A good example of such resistance occurred in Texas during October and November 1964 over biology textbooks adopted for use in the public schools. However, such opposition from fundamentalist groups arises every time any new textbooks come up for adoption, whether the subject matter is politics or religion. As a rule, the opponents of Charles Darwin are also against the United Nations or anything that might upset the *status quo.* Since some of the books in use were copyrighted in 1948, many teachers were requesting newer materials. Texas teachers, however, were not alone in requesting up-to-date materials.

In 1960 the American Institute of Biological Sciences had set up a curriculum study at the University of Colorado. The National Science Foundation had solicited the assistance of such groups and, five million dollars later, several books were published that met professional standards.

In October 1964 the Texas State Textbook Committee recommended that three of the new biology books be put on the approved list for use in the Texas schools. Immediately a protest was made, the Church of Christ being in the forefront of the attack; hence a hearing was requested. The three biology books were called anti-Christian, unscientific, and atheistic by one group of opponents that included a committee of four ministers, two out-of-state college professors, and two lawyers. Many of the two hundred who attended the hearing said that it resembled the 1925 "monkey trial" in Tennessee. They based their judgment on certain of the charges against evolution and the teaching of it. For example, some of the complaints ran as follows:

> These textbooks attempt to foist onto boys and girls an unproven theory. Boys and girls who do not believe in this theory are discriminated against. The theory of evolution is a materialistic theory. A being who springs from an amoeba has no soul in him. Evolution makes no provision for the resurrection of the soul. (An editor of a religious publication.)
>
> The theory of evolution undermines faith in God. It is atheistic. (A minister.)
>
> In addition to being unscientific, the evolution theory is also anti-Christian, for it contradicts the Genesis account of creation, the fall of man and the redemption of man from that fall by Christ. (A leader in the anti-evolution group.)
>
> Fundamental Bible-believing Christians think there is a great deal wrong with believing in evolution. . . . We believe the account of creation in the Book of Genesis to be a historical fact and that the teaching of evolution is a direct contradiction to the belief. (A minister.) [11]

Jack Binion, a member of the board of education, asked several of the witnesses who had led the assault upon the three books why they felt the board should take their recommendation above national science groups, the state textbook committee, and the commissioner of education—all experts in the field of educational material and knowledgeable as far as the books were concerned.[12] Though his query was unanswered, those in opposition did not withdraw their objection to the recommendations. They left the meeting, defeated to be sure, and went back to their homes and communities to await another issue. Fundamentalism in Texas—in the South—has never been famous for its silence and timidity. A member of the Texas house of representatives in 1973 introduced a bill requiring that whenever the Darwinian theory of evolution is discussed in the public schools equal time be given for a presentation of the Genesis account of creation. A similar bill was sponsored in the Georgia legislature a few months earlier.

Followers of the old-time religion have found many issues that have brought their forces out in full strength. A good example is the attack on the validity of the Revised Standard Version of the Bible, which was published in 1952. M. Luther Hux, pastor of the Temple Baptist Church in Rocky Mount, North Carolina, called a mass meeting of Baptists in November 1952 to protest the elimination of the word "virgin" from the RSV at Isa. 7:14. Hux declared that he would hold a public burning of the book, and some four hundred persons gathered from about ten different places to express their sympathy with him in his indignation. Hux, a missionary Baptist, had departed from the Southern Baptist Convention in 1946 in protest against certain tendencies toward "modernism" within his denomination. Luther A. Weigle, dean emeritus of the Yale Divinity School, and Kyle M. Yates, then pastor of the Second Baptist Church of Houston, Texas, who participated in the preparation of the new translation, were objects of this and similar attacks for "contaminating the Word of God," as the opponents to the RSV phrased their criticism. Although the principal objection was to the substitution of "young woman" for "virgin," there were other bones of contention. For example, Hux charged that in dialogue addressed to Jesus the use of the pronouns "you" and "your" instead of "thou" and "thy" denies "every basic concept of our historic Christian faith and destroys faith in the divine inspiration of the Scriptures; the essential deity of Jesus Christ; the resurrection of the body and the second personal coming of Christ." Kyle Yates' reply indicates that he was out of patience with all of this objection to the RSV: "It's disgusting to think of anyone's wanting to burn any version of the Bible." Yates added: "If he [Hux] would spend more time getting people to read the Bible instead of creating opposition and trying to burn it, he would be performing his duty much better." [13] Thus we see that intradenominational disputes, so prevalent in antebellum days, continue in our own times.

While one small group may engage in a destructive ritual such as book-burning, another may pursue another extreme. At the First Baptist Church of Pearland, Texas, a "Bibliothon" was scheduled, to last from sixty to sixty-five hours. A group assembled under a magnolia tree outside the church, and each person read the Bible aloud for thirty minutes, the rotation continuing without interruption until all sixty-six books were finished. The precedent for such a ritual was established in earlier times when the first books of the Bible were lost for decades in the rubble of the temple at Jerusalem. When they were recovered, a public reading was conducted to acquaint the people with the Scriptures. A spiritual awakening was the result. Hoping to set off such an awakening in his community through the "Bibliothon," the minister of the Pearland church commented: "The Bible is virtually a lost book in the average American home today. We want to get it back into our minds and hearts and then communicate it effectively to others." [14]

Although many social historians believe that this older religiousness, which helped establish a Southern way of life, a distinctive set of attitudes and philosophies, is in a twilight stage, certain traditions remain that are resistant to change. In a sense, the evangelical type of faith described in these pages has contributed to the existence of certain psychological reactions and hostility to outside influences in the realm of politics, economics, and sociology. Views on party loyalty, federal aid, and racism are involved. Awareness that the Southern character has been shaped by these traditions prompted sociology professor Earl Brewer of Emory University to warn board members of the National Council of Churches: "Churches in the Bible belt are going to have to break away from Southern tradition to retain moral leadership in the region." He explained that they would have to repudiate much of what they once sanctioned, in the name of the same gospel. For the Bible Belt to assume its role in a new era, its critics affirm, the Southern mind and spirit must be liberated from the carefully guarded and well-fortified sanctuaries created by an early nineteenth century folk.

10

Reflections
on the Bible Belt Mystique

ONE DOES NOT NECESSARILY write a book to solve a
problem, but to state it and make it real. So in the interest of clarification we shall add a few final reflections
on the content of Southern religion in its early stage,
along with certain observations regarding its effects,
difficult as they may be to support statistically.

As to content, the religion of the early South contained both the rational and the emotional. The sermons and religious periodicals reflected a theological
concern for the doctrine of God and the doctrine of
man. The researcher discovers an interest in definitions
and proofs of the existence of God, interpretations and
defenses of the Trinity, the attributes of the Deity, the
theory of creation and its relation to contemporary
knowledge, and divine providence (free will and original sin). He will find frequent explanations of the two-
fold nature of Christ, the Mediator and Redeemer, predestination (grace, election, perseverance of the saints,
and atonement), baptism, closed communion, the immortality of the soul, heaven, hell, death, the resurrection, the judgment, and the millennium. Herein is contained the hard core of much that was discussed and
argued with the primary objective of saving souls rather
than improving social conditions. The secondary goal
was to cut down denominations with rival beliefs in

order to win control and power in the community. Presbyterians and Episcopalians frequently found themselves doing battle along a broad theological front with Methodists and Baptists, when the latter groups were not preoccupied in confrontation with one another.

Fashion and taste prevail in religion as well as in clothing, architecture, or music. In colonial New England, theological speculation and Scriptural exposition were enjoyed by both pulpit and communicants, as the Scripturally documented sermons and copious notes recorded by the congregation seem to testify. The legalists of the eighteenth century gave way to the moralists of the nineteenth. The South experienced these transitions more rapidly because of the anti-intellectualism in the sparsely settled region. Particularly in the agrarian sector served by Methodists and Baptists, the people demanded excitement rather than thinking. These people reveled in popular discourses that appealed to their sympathies and passions, that carried the congregations on tours of deathbed and graveyard, to visit helpless widows and starving children in orphanages, and to behold the brutish alcoholic abusing the hysterical mother and helpless children. Though the era was predominantly evangelical, the reader should be reminded that the traditional topics also continued to be discussed before Southern congregations. Predestination, natural depravity, freedom of the will, and baptism were discussed, not in the context of the standard writings on these subjects, but the preachers' own interpretations of the Biblical passages. In the more thickly settled areas, where the ministers were more formally educated, the tools of religious scholarship were used but perhaps had little refining influence upon the behavior and thinking of the "coonskin" race of men.

The older, emotional type of religion had its greatest influence upon the common man. Historians cite the camp meetings and revivals that swept large regions of the rural Southland. Some observers went so far as to affirm that one of the major causes of emotional disorders, aside from monotonous labor and loneliness, was this peculiar brand of primitive and frequently violent worship.

In an address entitled "The Forgotten Man," delivered in June 1897 at the State Normal and Industrial School for Women at Greensboro, North Carolina, Walter Hines Page discusses the role of the politician and preacher in the educational development of the early South.[1] He refers to the preacher as "a mighty man in our life." He pays tribute to the type of preacher described earlier in these pages, referring to him as "an heroic man, a man who had all the qualities of the pioneer." Page adds:

> He was ready any day to face the hardships of the wilderness or to stand in the presence of the Almighty. I doubt if we have ever produced other men as great as our pioneer preachers. They were cast in so large a mould, they dealt so directly with the fundamental emotions of men and with some of the great facts of the spiritual life, that they almost ranged themselves with the giants. I had rather have known one of these men than all the political and military heroes that we have since bred. The politician has been the greater popular hero, but the preacher has had much the greater influence. For a century he was by far our greatest man—the man of the largest original power and of the strongest character. He inherited the heroic qualities of the pioneers, and he led a life at once serene and active. He was a primitive sort of character, genuine and fearless. If our traditions overrate the political leaders that we have produced, they as greatly underrate the early preachers.

Page wisely observes that the political leaders helped establish an aristocratic or class conception of education, which did not touch the masses. The people were led to believe that education was a special privilege—unattainable and unnecessary; consequently they remained in an illiterate state and a stationary social condition. The politician praised the common man—"the forgotten man"—for virtues he did not possess, deluding him, for the sake of control, into the belief that "he lived in the best State in the Union," that "the other politician had some harebrained plan to increase his taxes," and that he should beware of anyone who wished to bring about change. That is, "what was good enough for his fathers was good enough for him."

The preacher complemented the admonitions of this stump orator with a similar but more convincing line of reasoning. He told the common man that "the ills and misfortunes of this life were blessings in disguise, that God meant his poverty as a means of grace, and that if he accepted the right creed all would be well with him." Thus social inertia and stagnation resulted. This was his legacy.

But women, even more than men, became the victims of these two spokesmen for the *status quo*. They were, writes Page,

> thin and wrinkled in youth from ill prepared food, clad without warmth or grace, living in untidy houses, working from daylight till bed-time at the dull round of weary duties, the slaves of men of equal slovenliness, the mothers of joyless children—all uneducated if not illiterate.

The religion a Southern woman gleaned from these male chauvinist evangelists proved to be devastating because it taught her to endure hardships as preparation for the next world. Unlike the man, she found no escape in this life, enslaved by a social system that had God's blessing.

However, many of the early preachers were remarkable men, as these pages have testified, and they had an indelible influence upon their section. These circuit riders and farmer preachers dismounted after the Civil War and draped their mantles around the new species of religious leader of the late nineteenth and early twentieth century. But as these pages also reveal, the breed is not extinct. James Morris in a recent book, *The Preacher,* points out that the radio exhorters and tent-show evangelists are still very much in evidence throughout America, especially in the South and Southwest. There are others, like Billy Graham and Oral Roberts, whom Walter Hines Page would call "heroic men."

To be sure, the old-time religion has been greatly modified since the early days. It no longer has the mass appeal that it did, but sufficient evidence has been presented to illustrate that the older type of religiousness is not dead. In fact, a great many Southerners are turning to a type of neofundamentalism, probably as an insulation from social turmoil, an energy crisis, economic chaos, environmental pollution, international conflict, and the like. In a search for simple answers to complex problems, they have turned to the Bible for help. What is sought has been referred to by the more orthodox as the "plain truth." In this sense the older faith endures, and not only in the South.

The brush arbors and tents are disappearing and being replaced by air-conditioned auditoriums, but much of the fervor remains, particularly among certain of the minor sects and some Southern Baptists. The existence of blue laws, local option on liquor sales, objection to Darwin's theory, and intolerance toward such religious liberals as Unitarians and Universalists give evidence that pockets of the older attitudes persist. But the emergence of social action, a diminished fear of the Roman Catholic Church, and greater desegregation suggest that change is also occurring.

A revival of interest in religion among college students may seem to imply that the old-time faith is coming back to the campus, but this is not quite the case because much of the participation is outside the institution of the church. The fundamentalist Campus Crusade for Christ, Jesus Freak groups and Children of God are possible exceptions. There is a great deal of interest in Oriental mysticism, transcendental meditation, Zen, etc., but these represent new trends and experimentation.

At the risk of oversimplification, this author affirms that Southern religion primarily demanded that the individual be able to declare the "time when and the place where" his new birth began. Hence, the central claim in Southern evangelical Christianity is contained in the simple statement, "Ye must be born again." As the early chapters illustrated, this rebirth began with single individuals and set off chain reactions in the community, developing into a sectional holocaust. Methodist and Baptist preachers effectively dramatized the tragedy of Jesus. "It is perfectly matched to the Southern mystique, to the Southerner's tragic sentimentality," Marshall Frady wisely observes.[2] Although he is specifically characterizing the Southern Baptist, the concept is applicable to most rural people who played such key roles in this early religious drama. Frady writes:

> Christ is, in this religious sensibility, a figure of melancholy sweetness, with a tragic bearded face strikingly like those thin doomed faces of young Confederate officers that peer out of flecked tintypes. The poignancy of Jesus to the Southerner is that He consented to become human, that from the moment of His birth He was divinity crucified on the cross of flesh, and that He did all this—of unbearable sweetness!—for the sake 'of a wretch like me.'[3]

This melodramatic theme endures in revival hymns that were popular in evangelical Christianity in the

nineteenth century and it reverberates in the twentieth.
For believers in the old-time religion, the ghost of the
Confederate dead is an inseparable legacy, part of their
subconsciousness, because of the supreme sacrifice
made individually and collectively by the men in gray.
The spirit of Jesus is also part of this same subconsciousness because of his martyrdom. Although orthodox Southerners will grant that Christ died on
Golgotha, not at Gettysburg or Appomattox, his death
too was heroic. Deep within the Southern psyche is the
belief that there will be a resurrection—real or symbolic—and an unconscious awareness that the ghosts of
yesterday form a holy alliance in the Bible Belt. One
aspect of the Southern mystique unfolds when the congregation sings:

> Faith of our fathers! living still
>   In spite of dungeon, fire, and sword,
> O how our hearts beat high with joy
>   Whene'er we hear that glorious word:
> Faith of our fathers, holy faith!
> We will be true to thee till death.

But we cannot part even on the triumphant note of
this hymn without some obiter dicta. The intent of this
book has been primarily to explain and describe Southern orthodoxy in a historical context with observations
of some of its manifestations in the twentieth century.
No explicit effort was made to evaluate this older pietism; yet the perceptive reader will recognize that the
author's point of view intrudes at many points. And
now the temptation is great to point out weakness and
evidence of obsolescence in the religion that has been
described. If we are to prove any weaknesses, however,
these must necessarily be demonstrated through their
effect upon the Southern region—upon its collective
behavior. As far as the individual is concerned, he has
to make his own value judgment as to the type of faith

best suited to his intellectual, cultural, and social standing. He hopes to be a credit to society and at the same time to fulfill his own expectations. Certainly his religious beliefs will be a catalyst in the total performance. Perhaps the following observations may be of interest to some who have observed that the South has resisted the general process of Americanization. This older pietism has surely played a part in shaping the behavior and thought of the region.

First, let us look at the role of religion in *the issue of the Negro and slavery* and maybe some will understand why in the 1960's black militants stormed into Southern churches uttering defiant accusations and demanding financial reimbursement for two centuries of oppression and exploitation. Militants have further charged that Southern religionists were instrumental in dehumanizing slaves and in setting them apart from white society. The basis for all these accusations will have to be examined historically.

Briefly, Virginia planters in the seventeenth century found themselves in conflict with their priests. The planters were unwilling to accept the traditional assumption that Christianity and freedom were synonymous. They feared that the institution of slavery would be destroyed if such an assumption were allowed, for a baptized Christian would automatically become a human being and entitled to his freedom. The planters had been laboring with the concept that human beings could not be enslaved. The Virginia Assembly in 1667 resolved the whole controversy that had existed among Anglicans by affirming that baptism had no effect upon the status of bondage or freedom. Therefore, a slave could now become a baptized Christian but would remain in his subhuman position as merely property or chattel. Yet he was granted certain burial rites and the hope for an afterlife.

Slavery, then, came to be viewed by many Virginians

in a favorable light because it introduced heathens to the white man's culture and to Christianity, thus contributing to their ultimate salvation, prospects unavailable to them in their original state of existence in Africa. This was the same general position taken by the Puritans three decades earlier in their religious sanction of slavery: Negroes, a debased people, should be enslaved to bring them within the reach of God's grace. They also viewed the Indian in the same light.

In time other denominations came to share the Anglican's view of slavery, but not without considerable agony of spirit. On a regional basis the struggle fell into two stages.

Prior to 1830 the South was wrestling internally with its problem. Strong humanitarian groups were expounding the dreams of men like Thomas Jefferson, who believed that slavery was utterly inconsistent with the law of God. But the invention of the cotton gin led to a fabulous increase in cotton production, and slavery now became a regional concern. Fears arose that the Southern economy could not absorb the nearly two million freed Negroes, also that racial problems would arise when races so different were brought together in a free society, with the liberated race far outnumbering whites in most areas.

After 1830, the South became increasingly proslavery as a result of the irritating activities of abolitionists. Religionists and politicians now joined ranks in support of this "peculiar institution." Senator John C. Calhoun was joined by a galaxy of intelligentsia such as Albert Taylor Bledsoe, George Fitzhugh, William J. Grayson, William Gilmore Simms, and Thomas Cooper in treatises designed to show that slavery was a positive good. The arguments were many in support of preserving the system: (1) both Scriptures and history justify slavery; (2) the national economy would suffer if the cotton industry were curtailed; (3) racial trouble would result if two peoples unprepared culturally and socially were rushed suddenly into fraternization on an equal basis; (4) property rights would be endangered; (5) the principle of "states rights" as provided in the constitution would be violated.

The seventeenth-century view expressed earlier now came to be heard more and more. Just as the early Puritans looked upon the devil as a black man so the Calvinists in the South viewed the Negro, recently from a heathen world, as an inferior and corrupt specimen of humanity. James McBride Dabbs, in his book *Who Speaks for the South?* explains that the Negro was close to the earth, was "an earth figure at work or rest, of the same dark color as earth, suited to black lands, deep forests, and mysterious, impenetrable swamps." [4] By association with religionists who so viewed the Negro, others of a slightly different theological strain, e.g., Arminians or Methodists, sharing a belief in original sin, also came to see the slave as not being thoroughly "washed in the Blood of the Lamb." Southern religion before the Civil War, then, provided an argument whereby whites could justify the system of slavery on the grounds of black inferiority; it also protected some from a sense of shame and guilt which was heard expressed by a few Confederate leaders when the tide of battle began to turn, but which did not surface among Southerners capable of possessing social consciousness until late in the nineteenth century, and significantly so only in the mid-twentieth.

This particular brand of emotionalism may be faulted in that it supported dehumanizing a vast segment of the population and advocated white supremacy. It provided a rationale for a pattern of thought that has led to a guilt complex and alienation of groups of people from one another. Certainly the institution of slavery was peculiar to the South, although beliefs in white supremacy existed in other sections of America. According to Allen

F. Stein and Thomas N. Walters, "It robbed the white man of his morality, for in depriving another man of his rights, he deprived himself of his own most precious birthright: his innocence and his human dignity." [5]

Another legacy of the Bible Belt mystique was the development of *a stubborn individualism*—self-reliant, opposed to the pressures of an organized society, touchy on a point of honor, resistant to change. The pickup truck equipped with gun rack and rifle symbolizes an attitude that prevails in the rural South but is not necessarily peculiar to that area. Many Protestants who participated in the outdoor meetings also demonstrated their individualistic traits when they made such a public spectacle of getting saved. There was little consideration for social justice or the betterment of society; instead, there was an emphasis only upon self-preservation, the kind of behavior reflected by a man escaping from a building in flames. However, these early Southerners were naïvely honest, aware of their individualistic, lawless, and sinful ways, eager to hear a hard, strict gospel—a sort of muscular Christianity—where an unlettered and rawboned spokesman for the divine would attack the devil, not with logic, but with bluster and clenched fists, drive him up in the corner and beat him into senseless submission. This was the kind of faith which became a motivating force behind the Redeemers and the Ku Klux Klan—law and order, one might say. But what effect do such expressions of individualism have upon the Southern image?

Related to the trait of individualism is *a syndrome of violence*—which is a legacy of slavery. There is no similarity here to the type of violence that occurred in Dallas on November 22, 1963, an incident that could have taken place anywhere else in America, as it did with the assassination of Robert Kennedy, and the attempted assassination of George Wallace. The murders of Martin Luther King, Jr., in Memphis and of the Freedom Riders in Mississippi are something else—examples of the type of violence in question, uniquely Southern in motivation. The kind of emotionalism described in these pages has also been the fountainhead of various types of sex crimes, persecution, and neurotic behavior.

In Chapter 2 reference was made to the three "Ghosts" that haunted Southern states in the late nineteenth century—"the Ghost of the Confederate dead, the Ghost of religious orthodoxy, and the Ghost of [the fear of] Negro domination." United, these phantoms helped create a political and religious solidarity. Their symbols became the Confederate flag, emotional Christianity, and Jim Crowism. Unlike the ghost of Prince Hamlet's father that frequented the Castle of Elsinore, these specters have haunted not only the Southern landscape but also the heart of the Southerner himself. They isolate the individual and build up a barrier between his society and the rest of America. That is,

> there is a *sine qua non* for the South—there is a thing of the mind, a matter of character and a point of view— which marks a Southerner, which marks the best of the Southerners and used to mark more. It is a thing, maybe, which even in the South is disappearing; but only in the South now does it move even thinly over the land and in those men who once knew the land. It is in the sum and vestige of all those facts that have been recognized as *the lost cause, the Southern temper, Bible-belt religion, redneck mentality, the Mind of the South.*[6]

Certainly this older religion has played a significant role in creating an inflexible defense of the *status quo*.

Another trait of the Southerner is a *reverence for the past.* With the economic and political loss of the Civil War, and the racial humiliations that followed, "this healthy respect for the past was enormously intensified and became a religious force in the South." Customs and traditions became sacred, replacing the forward-looking power of ideals.[7] Dabbs explains the problem in the framework of the type of religion presented in the pages of this book when he quotes an uncle who died in 1914: "Ideals are a sin, Alice. We should love God." That is, God was visible in all the facts of the world. If God was going anywhere, that was God's business. From all indications, Southerners were certainly not going anywhere, maybe moving half consciously with the drift of things.[8] The Southerner's type of religiousness resulted in a static society, an inability to challenge fate, to conquer it, to escape the prison walls and get into the mainstream of history. Human perfectibility, the idea of progress, and the American Dream were not in the Southerner's consciousness. He knew not economic abundance, success or victory, freedom or innocence.[9] Original sin became almost a genetic reality rather than a theological affirmation. Shame and guilt lay deep in the psyche, thus they became the burdens of Southern history.

Another influence of evangelical Christianity—upon the Southerner's *love of the land, and place, and emphasis upon family ties* would have to be explained in terms of the personal nature of the religion. Life itself "tended to be personal, mainly a matter of strong individuals, or loyal family groups, in a largely unstructured world, constantly changing under the fact of the frontier.[10] The frontier revivals and outdoor meetings described in these pages are illustrative of this personal quality. Before the War, Southerners came to see their cause as God's, the South as His favorite soil. As the South's social order and its religion were united, a universal God was replaced by a tribal God whose tribe consisted of the white race, to which blacks "were attached as hewers of wood and drawers of water." [11] The love of place came to be regarded as God's sacred place, and the defense of this land took on a spiritual significance. Members of a family were united in a type of crusade. Together they felt secure. They had been brought together in a common effort, resisting a Satanic force, and sharing common heroes—members of their tribe or clan. The theme of "Blest Be the Tie" became the family's source of inspiration—binding them together in their common effort and even giving assurance of a reunion in the life to come. The inevitable result of such a faith is that it provides guidance and rationalization for those involved in a lost cause. It seems to be more a preparation for death than a preparation for life.

A close affinity of politics and religion in the South is another legacy of this religion. The early part of the nineteenth century began to reflect interrelationships. Political solidarity was conceived in an atmosphere of religious tension. Within the Presbyterian church as early as 1837 a conflict arose over cardinal points in the Westminster confession (a definition of the covenant with respect to atonement) that resulted in a division that created the Old School and the New School. This theological controversy led to a separation of the denomination into two groups, later divided along sectional lines. In the Methodist Church the split occurred in a meeting of the Georgia conference in 1844 over the Bishop Andrew case, when Southern religionists refused to allow the bishop to yield to Northern pressure and free his slaves. Thus the Methodist Episcopal Church South emerged over a political issue. Baptists (divided first on the issue of universal redemption versus limited redemption—the old doctrine of election) began looking at the economic, cultural, and social differences between the two sections of the country. The rift in their denomination became decisive. Thus the Southern churches helped prepare the way for schisms among religionists and also prepared the way for Southern political solidarity leading up to the Civil

War. The older pietism for a long time resisted efforts toward reunion of Northern and Southern denominations. A number of splits remain to this day.

Attention has already been called to *the preoccupation of emotionalism with moralism.* Rules abound concerning Sabbath observance, intemperance, the use of tobacco, dancing, card-playing, and theater-attending—so-called vices in the nineteenth century. In the South today many religious groups still consider some common amusements as sinful and make quite a thing of the least infraction. Some psychologists and psychiatrists fault the older pietism for its unwholesome view of sex and attribute many mental health and domestic problems to the attitudes derived from a distorted religious training in childhood.

An illustration from the author's childhood will speak for itself. Following a summer revival meeting, the only recreation center in Bonham, Texas, was leveled and filled in with dirt as a result of the diabolical eloquence of a firebrand who convinced the community that "anybody who would expose herself [or himself] in a bathing suit in public would go to hell and anybody who looked at her wouldn't be far behind." He added: "The devil is running that swimming hole. God has nothing to do with it. Fill it up and run the devil out of Bonham." When the center was closed, the young people returned to the monotonous routine that often plagued small towns in the 1920's.

Willie Morris in his *North Toward Home* cites an experience as a child in Yazoo, Mississippi:

> One of the preachers at a church at the edge of town, Brother L—, gave a sermon one Sunday entitled, "Why Do We Wear Clothes?" His point was that we wear clothes to keep from being naked and ashamed, because our bodies are shameful and should be hidden. He got so hacked up on this subject, beating the pulpit with his knuckles, rolling his eyes to the ceiling, that I began

worrying as I sat as a good visitor in his church if my own wardrobe was sufficient to last out the winter.[12]

Then Morris explains that a few weeks later Brother L— was caught by some of the church ladies in the Sunday School basement with a schoolteacher late one night under circumstances that contradicted the theme of this sermon. Morris was illustrating the point that a religion like Brother L—'s did not seem attractive to the young people and puzzled them with its inconsistencies.

Another characteristic of the older emotionalism, experienced by countless young people in the South— and in other parts of America as well, no doubt—was *its seasonal crusade to save a soul.* Morris writes:

> Before I turned twelve, I had been "saved" not once, but at least a dozen times. I had played, at various times in church pageants, kings, wisemen, angels, shepherds, camel-drivers, Joseph, and Jesus. I had given away enough frankincense and myrrh to stock the cosmetics counter in a modest-sized nickel-and-dime store, and I had tried to get into so many inns where there was no more room that I would have done better to take out a long-term American Express Credit Card acceptable at all hostelries in the Middle East.[13]

He observes that this simple small-town type of faith begins to wear thin as a boy gets older, not mainly because he grows more intelligent or experienced from the outside world, but because he becomes bored with it all.

Anyone who makes passing remarks about the old-time faith must be aware that in the realm of religion, mankind has generally been hostile to innovation. It is an area in which one can always start an argument without too much effort. With this thought, the author is reminded of Sir William Drummond's epigram that concludes his *Academical Questions:* "He who will not reason is a bigot; he who cannot is a fool, and he who dare not is a slave." So the author can only hope that those not included in one of these three categories will find this book, else he has wasted his time.

Notes

An Aside to the Reader

1. *The Complete Works of Benjamin Franklin,* ed. by John Bigelow (G. P. Putnam's Sons, 1888), Vol. IX, pp. 354–355.

Chapter 1

The Nature of the Old-Time Religion

1. William G. McLoughlin, Jr., *Modern Revivalism: Charles Grandison Finney to Billy Graham* (The Ronald Press Co., 1959), pp. 466–467.

2. R. Nevitt Sandford, "Ethnocentrism in Relation to Some Religious Attitudes and Practice," in Theodor W. Adorno *et al., The Authoritarian Personality* (Harper & Brothers, 1950), p. 219.

3. See H. Richard Niebuhr, *The Social Sources of Denominationalism* (Henry Holt & Company, 1929), for a reasonable explanation of the rationale behind denominational affiliations in the United States.

4. Samuel A. Stouffer, *Communism, Conformity, and Civil Liberties: A Cross-Section of the Nation Speaks Its Mind* (Doubleday & Company, Inc., 1955).

5. H. Shelton Smith, *In His Image, but . . . Racism in Southern Religion, 1780–1910* (Duke University Press, 1972).

6. Richard Hofstadter, *Anti-Intellectualism in American Life* (Alfred A. Knopf, Inc., 1963), p. 133.

7. Cf. McLoughlin, *Modern Revivalism,* pp. 466–467.

8. T. E. Hulme, *Speculations: Essays on Humanism and the Philosophy of Art* (Harcourt, Brace and Company, Inc., 1924), pp. 50–51.

9. See Reinhold Niebuhr, "The Impact of Protestantism Today," *Atlantic Monthly*, Vol. CLXXXI, February 1948, pp. 59–62.

Chapter 2

THE BEGINNINGS OF SOUTHERN RELIGIOUSNESS

1. George Stanley Godwin, *The Great Revivalists* (Beacon Press, Inc., 1951), p. 21.

2. Philip Schaff, *America: A Sketch of the Political, Social and Religious Character of the United States of North America, in Two Lectures* (New York: C. Scribner, 1855), p. 176.

3. James Porter, *A Compendium of Methodism* (Boston: C. H. Peirce and Co., 1851), p. 173.

4. Henry Kallock Rowe, *The History of Religion in the United States* (The Macmillan Company, 1928), p. 75; cf. William Warren Sweet, *Revivalism in America: Its Origin, Growth, and Decline* (Charles Scribner's Sons, 1944).

5. John M. Peck, "Thoughts and Suggestions on Revivals of Religion," *Western Baptist Review*, Vol. IV (1849), p. 308.

6. J. H. Spencer, *A History of Kentucky Baptists from 1769 to 1885* . . . (Cincinnati, 1886), Vol. I, p. 498.

7. James Gallaher, *The Western Sketch-Book* (Boston: Crocker and Brewster, 1852), pp. 29–30. For a background of the liberal thought or irreligiousness one will find of interest the following: H. M. Morais, *Deism in Eighteenth Century America* (Columbia University Press, 1934); J. M. Robertson, *A History of Freethought in the Nineteenth Century*, 2 vols. (London: Watts and Co., 1929).

8. Charles A. Johnson, *The Frontier Camp Meeting, Religion's Harvest Time* (Southern Methodist University Press, 1955), p. 204.

9. Robert Davidson, *History of the Presbyterian Church in the State of Kentucky* (New York: Carter, 1847), p. 131.

10. Merton E. Coulter, *College Life in the Old South* (The Macmillan Company, 1928), p. 193.

11. Peter Cartwright, *The Autobiography of Peter Cartwright, the Backwoods Preacher* (Cincinnati: Cranston and Curts, 1856), p. 24.

12. Charles Crossfield Ware, *Barton W. Stone, Pathfinder of Christian Union: A Story of His Life and Times* . . . (The Bethany Press, 1932), p. 77; quoted from Josiah Espy, *Memoranda of a Tour*, p. 24.

13. Davidson, *History of the Presbyterian Church* . . . , p. 131.

14. Spencer, *A History of Kentucky Baptists* . . . , Vol. I, p. 50.

15. T. C. Blake, *The Old Log House: A History and Defense of the Cumberland Presbyterian Church* (Nashville: Cumberland Presbyterian Church, 1879), p. 20.

16. Robert B. Semple, *A History of the Rise and Progress of the Baptists in Virginia* (Richmond: John Lynch, 1810), p. 208.

17. Spencer, *A History of Kentucky Baptists* . . . , Vol. I, p. 175.

18. James Smith (ed.), *The Posthumous Works of the Reverend and Pious M'Gready* . . . *Late Minister of the Gospel* . . . (Louisville: W. W. Worsley, 1831–1833), Vol. I, p. ix.

19. T. Marshall Smith, *Legends of the War of Independence, and of the West* (Louisville: J. F. Brennan, 1855), p. 373.

20. *Ibid.*, p. 376; cf. Henry Howe, *Historical Collections of the Great West* . . . (Cincinnati: Henry Howe, 1856), pp. 204–206.

21. "History of a Church in the South," *A Series of Tracts on the Doctrines, Order, and Polity of the Presbyterian Church in the United States of America* . . . , Vol. III (n.d.), p. 260.

22. Gallaher, *The Western Sketch-Book*, p. 32.

Chapter 3

THE ERUPTION OF SALVATION

1. Smith, *Legends* . . . , p. 377.

2. D. Sullins, *Recollections of an Old Man, Seventy Years*

in Dixie, 1827–1897 (Bristol, Tenn.: The King Printing Co., 1910), pp. 33–34.

3. Spencer, A History of Kentucky Baptists . . . , Vol. I, p. 693.

4. Timothy Flint, A Condensed Geography and History of the Western States, or the Mississippi Valley (Cincinnati: B. H. Flint, 1826), Vol. I, pp. 220–221.

5. Davidson, History of the Presbyterian Church . . . , p. 136.

6. Ibid., p. 138 (quoted from the Gospel Herald, Vol. II, p. 200).

7. Gallaher, The Western Sketch-Book, p. 42.

8. Sweet, Revivalism in America . . . , p. 131. Sweet adds: "There was never any legislation concerning it; the name 'camp meeting' does not occur in any of the General Conference Indices. There are no rules in the Discipline to govern it."

9. Spencer, A History Kentucky Baptists . . . , Vol. I, p. 563.

10. Ibid., Vol. I, p. 564.

11. F. D. Srygley, Seventy Years in Dixie, Recollections, Sermons and Sayings of T. W. Caskey and Others (Nashville: Gospel Advocate Publishing Co., 1891), pp. 222–223.

12. Thomas L. Nichols, Forty Years of American Life (London: John Maxwell and Co., 1864), Vol. I, p. 79.

13. James Flint, Letters from America, 1818–1820 (Reuben Gold Thwaites [ed.], Early Western Travels 1748–1846, Vol. IX; Cleveland: Arthur H. Clark Co., 1904), p. 258.

14. Richard McNemar, The Kentucky Revival; or, A Short History of the Late Extraordinary Outpouring of the Spirit of God in the Western States of America (New York: Edward C. Jenkins, 1846), pp. 25–26.

15. Flint, Letters from America . . . , p. 259.

16. Nichols, Forty Years of American Life, Vol. I, p. 81.

17. Flint, Letters from America . . . , p. 262.

18. Ibid., pp. 263–264.

19. Albea Godbold, The Church College of the Old South (Duke University Press, 1944), pp. 128–130; cf. Sweet, Revivalism in America . . . , p. 119.

20. Gallaher, The Western Sketch-Book, p. 33.

21. John Rogers and Barton Warren Stone, The Biography

of *Barton Warren Stone, Written by Himself* (1853), p. 39.
22. *Ibid.*
23. *Ibid.*
24. Davidson, *History of the Presbyterian Church* . . . ,
p. 143.
25. *Ibid.*, p. 144.
26. *Ibid.*
27. Gallaher, *The Western Sketch-Book*, p. 33.
28. Davidson, *History of the Presbyterian Church* . . . ,
p. 145.
29. McNemar, *The Kentucky Revival* . . . , p. 35.
30. Cartwright, *The Autobiography* . . . , pp. 48–49; cf.
Rogers and Stone, *The Biography of Barton Warren Stone*
. . . , p. 40.
31. Jo C. Guild, *Old Times in Tennessee, with Historical,
Personal, and Political Scraps and Sketches* (Nashville:
Tavel, Eastman and Howell, 1878), p. 42.
32. Cartwright, *The Autobiography* . . . , pp. 50–51.
33. McNemar, *The Kentucky Revival* . . . , p. 65.
34. T. C. Anderson, *Life of Rev. George Donnell* (Nashville: Southern Methodist Publishing House, 1859), pp.
69–70.
35. *Biblical Repertory and Princeton Review* (New York:
G. & C. Carvill), n.s., Vol. VI (1877), p. 339.
36. Lorenzo Dow, *History of Cosmopolite; or, The Writings of Rev. Lorenzo Dow, Containing His Experiences, and
Travels in Europe and America* . . . (Cincinnati: Robert
Clarke and Co., 1870), p. 184.
37. *Ibid.*
38. McNemar, *The Kentucky Revival* . . . , p. 64; also Davidson, *History of the Presbyterian Church* . . . , p. 150.
39. Rogers and Stone, *The Biography of Barton Warren
Stone* . . . , p. 41.
40. McNemar, *The Kentucky Revival* . . . , p. 63.
41. *Ibid.* Cf. Davidson, *History of the Presbyterian
Church* . . . , p. 151; Rogers and Stone, *The Biography of
Barton Warren Stone* . . . , p. 40.
42. *Biblical Repertory*, Vol. VI, p. 339.
43. Rogers and Stone, *The Biography of Barton Warren
Stone* . . . , p. 41.
44. David Benedict, *A General History of the Baptist De-*

nomination in America, and Other Parts of the World . . .
(Boston: Lincoln and Edmonds, 1813), Vol. II, p. 256.
  45. Davidson, *History of the Presbyterian Church* . . . ,
p. 152. Cf. McNemar, *The Kentucky Revival* . . . , pp. 66–67.
  46. Rogers and Stone, *The Biography of Barton Warren
Stone* . . . , p. 41.
  47. *Ibid.*, pp. 41–42.
  48. Davidson, *History of the Presbyterian Church* . . . ,
p. 154 (Note).
  49. Spencer, *A History of Kentucky Baptists* . . . , Vol. I,
p. 505.
  50. A. W. Putnam, *History of Middle Tennessee; or, Life
and Times of Gen. James Robertson* (Nashville: A. A. Stitt,
Southern Methodist Publishing House, 1859), pp. 311–312.
  51. Anderson, *Life of Rev. George Donnell* . . . , p. 73.
  52. *A Geographical, Historical, Commercial and Agricul-
tural View of the United States of America* . . . (London:
Edwards and Knibb, 1820), p. 57.
  53. Johnson, *The Frontier Camp Meeting* . . . , p. 4.

Among the sources on Southern religion that the serious
student will find of interest are the following: Edwin Mc-
Neill Poteat, Jr., "Religion in the South," in William T.
Couch (ed.), *Culture in the South* (The University of North
Carolina Press, 1934); Timothy L. Smith, *Revivalism and Social Reform in Mid-Nineteenth-Century America* (Abingdon
Press, 1957); Alice Felt Tyler, *Freedom's Ferment: Phases of
American Social History to 1860* (The University of Min-
nesota Press, 1944); Bernard A. Weisberger, *They Gathered at
the River: The Story of the Great Revivalists and Their Im-
pact Upon Religion in America* (Little, Brown & Co., 1958).

Chapter 4

THE MAN IN THE PULPIT

  1. Thomas Hamilton, *Men and Manners in America* (Ed-
inburgh: William Blackwood, 1838), Vol. II, p. 395.
  2. Johnson, *The Frontier Camp Meeting* . . . , p. 113.
  3. Spencer, *A History of Kentucky Baptists* . . . , Vol. I,
p. 660.
  4. David Ramsey, *The History of South-Carolina, from*

Its First Settlement in 1670 to the Year 1808 (Charleston: David Longworth, 1809), Vol. II, p. 31 (note).

5. William Warren Sweet, *The Rise of Methodism in the West: Being the Journal of the Western Conference 1800–1811* (New York and Cincinnati: Methodist Book Concern, 1919), pp. 46–47.

6. Cartwright, *The Autobiography* . . . , p. 522.

7. *Ibid.*, p. 243.

8. Spencer, *A History of Kentucky Baptists* . . . , Vol. I, p. 194.

9. W. H. Venable, *Beginnings of Literary Culture in the Ohio Valley, Historical and Biographical Sketches* (Cincinnati: Robert Clarke and Co., 1891), pp. 215–216.

10. Edward Eggleston, *The Circuit Rider: A Tale of the Heroic Age* (New York: J. B. Ford and Co., 1874), p. 92.

11. *Ibid.*, pp. 102–103.

12. A. De Puy Van Buren, *Jottings of a Year's Sojourn in the South; or, First Impressions of the Country and Its People; with a Glimpse at School Teaching in that Southern Land, and Reminiscences of Distinguished Men* (Battle Creek, Mich.: Review and Herald Printers, 1859), p. 104.

13. T. A. S. Adams, *Enscotidion; or Shadow of Death*, ed. by Thomas O. Summers (Nashville: Southern Methodist Publishing House, 1876), Canto III, xii, 90.

14. Venable, *Beginnings of Literary Culture in the Ohio Valley* . . . , p. 335.

15. John A. Broadus, "Obey Your Parents," *Religious Herald* (1853), p. 115.

16. Henry Fowler, *The American Pulpit: Sketches, Biographical and Descriptive of Living American Preachers and of the Religious Movements and Distinctive Ideas Which They Represent* (New York: F. M. Fairchild and Co., 1856), p. 130.

17. Flint, *A Condensed Geography and History of the Western States* . . . , Vol. I, p. 219.

18. David Crockett, *Autobiography*, with an introduction by Hamlin Garland (Charles Scribner's Sons, 1923), pp. 247–248.

19. Amelia (Coppuck) Welby, "Pulpit Eloquence," *Poems* (New York: D. Appleton and Co., 1850), p. 181.

20. William Gilmore Simms, *Guy Rivers, A Tale of Georgia*

(New York: A. C. Armstrong and Son, 1882), p. 147.
    21. *Ibid.*, p. 151.
    22. From William Wirt, *The Letters of the British Spy* (1803), in *Southern Literature, 1579–1895*, ed. by Louise Manly (Richmond: B. F. Johnson Publishing Co., 1895), pp. 133–134.
    23. William Gilmore Simms, *Charlemont; or, The Pride of a Village, a Kentucky Tale* (New York: Redfield, 1856), p. 76.
    24. *Ibid.*, pp. 76–77.
    25. James Hall, *Sketches of History, Life, and Manners* (Philadelphia: Harrison Hall, 1835), Vol. I, p. 231.
    26. John C. Keener, *The Post-Oak Circuit* (Nashville, 1857), pp. 268–271.
    27. See James Truslow Adams (ed.), *Dictionary of American History* (Charles Scribner's Sons, 1940), Vol. III, p. 380. Also Hunter Dickinson Farish, *The Circuit Rider Dismounts, 1865–1900* (The Dietz Press, 1938).
    28. Simms, *Guy Rivers*, pp. 147–148.
    29. Paul Neff Garber, *The Methodist Meeting House* (New York: Editorial Department . . . the Methodist Church, 1941), p. 29.
    30. Simms, *Charlemont*, p. 75.
    31. John Esten Cooke, *The Virginia Comedians; or, Old Days in the Old Dominion* (New York: D. Appleton and Co., 1883), Vol. II, pp. 228–229.
    32. *Selections from the Miscellaneous Writings of George W. Bagby* (Richmond: Whittet and Shepperson, 1884), Vol. I, p. 144.

Chapter 5

THE SPIRIT OF SECTARIANISM

    1. William Warren Sweet, *The Story of Religion in America* (Harper & Brothers, 1930), p. 373.
    2. Jesse Laney Boyd, *A Popular History of the Baptists in Mississippi* (Jackson, Miss.: Baptist Press, 1930), p. 117.
    3. William Faux, *Memorable Days in America*, Vol. I (Reuben Gold Thwaites [ed.], *Early Western Travels, 1748–1846*, Vol. XI; Cleveland: Arthur H. Clark Co., 1904), p. 115.

4. Blake, *The Old Log House*, p. 21.

5. Hamilton, *Men and Manners in America*, Vol. II, pp. 397–398. Cf. Charles D. Drake, *Pioneer Life in Kentucky, a Series of Reminiscential Letters* . . . (Cincinnati: Robert Clarke and Co., 1870), p. 194. Also Spencer, *A History of Kentucky Baptists* . . . , Vol. I, p. 663.

6. Hamilton, *Men and Manners in America*, Vol. II, pp. 397–398.

7. Charles Murray, *Travels in North America During the Years 1834, 1835, and 1836* . . . (London: Richard Bentley, 1839), Vol. I, pp. 222–223.

8. Spencer, *A History of Kentucky Baptists* . . . , Vol. I, p. 663.

9. Schaff, *America* . . . , p. 113.

10. *Ibid.*

11. Ernest Hamlin Abbott, "Religious Life in America: New Tendencies in the Old South," *Outlook*, Vol. LXX (1902), p. 131.

12. Schaff, *America* . . . , p. 118.

13. *Ibid.*, p. 117.

14. E. DeForest Leach, "The Old Churches in the New South," *The Christian Century*, Vol. XLVI (1929), p. 1279.

15. Thomas Smyth, *Complete Works*, ed. by J. W. Flinn (Columbia, S.C.: R. L. Bryan Co., 1908), Vol. IX, p. 15.

16. Alexander Campbell, "Religious Controversy," *Millennial Harbinger*, Vol. I (1830), p. 41.

17. James King, "Controversy," *Calvinistic Magazine*, n.s., Vol. I (1846), p. 15.

18. *Ibid.*, p. 16.

19. Alexander Campbell, "Religious Controversy," *loc. cit.*, p. 42.

20. Smyth, *Complete Works*, Vol. IX, p. 16.

21. *Ibid.* Cf. "Spiritual Warfare," *Zion's Advocate*, Vol. VI (1859), p. 49. Also "Religious Controversy," *Zion's Advocate*, Vol. VI (1859), p. 212.

22. L. A. Lowry, *An Earnest Search for Truth in a Series of Letters from a Son to His Father* (Philadelphia: Presbyterian Board of Publication, 1852), pp. 65–66.

23. Robert Davidson, *History of the Presbyterian Church in the State of Kentucky*, p. 160.

24. Frances Trollope, *Domestic Manners of the Americans* (London: Wittaker, Treacher and Co., 1832), Vol. I, p. 110.

25. William Warren Sweet, *Religion on the American Frontier 1783–1840*, Vol. II, *The Presbyterians* . . . (Harper & Brothers, 1936), p. 89 (from Davidson, *History*, pp. 163, 164; Lyle MSS., pp. 47–48).

26. Walter Brownlow Posey, *The Development of Methodism in the Old Southwest, 1783–1824* (Tuscaloosa, Ala.: Weatherford Printing Co., 1933), p. 31.

27. John Lambert, *Travels Through Canada, and the United States of North America* . . . (London: Pickard Taylor and Co., 1813), Vol. II, pp. 271–272.

28. John Steinbeck, *The Grapes of Wrath* (The Viking Press, Inc., 1939), p. 29.

29. *Ibid.*, p. 30.

30. B. F. Riley, *A History of the Baptists in States East of the Mississippi* (Philadelphia: American Baptist Publication Society, 1898), p. 170.

31. Peter Cartwright, *Autobiography*, p. 80.

32. Hosea Holcombe, *A History of the Rise and Progress of the Baptists in Alabama* (Philadelphia: King and Baird, 1840), p. 266 (note).

33. Riley, *A History of the Baptists* . . . , p. 170.

34. Spencer, *A History of Kentucky Baptists* . . . , Vol. I, pp. 646–647.

35. Walter Brownlow Posey, *Religious Strife on the Southern Frontier* (Baton Rouge: Louisiana State University Press, 1965), p. 21.

36. *Ibid.*, pp. 58–60.

37. Cf. *ibid.*, pp. 76–112.

38. Joseph B. Cobb, *Mississippi Scenes; or, Sketches of Southern and Western Life and Adventure* . . . (Philadelphia: A. Hart, Late Carey and Hart, 1851), pp. 17–19.

Chapter 6

THE CRUSADE AGAINST LIBERALISM

1. William Meade, *Old Churches, Ministers and Families of Virginia* (Philadelphia: J. B. Lippincott and Co., 1857), Vol. II, p. 235.

2. Clement Eaton, *The Freedom of Thought Struggle in the Old South* (Durham: Duke University Press, 1940), pp. 13–14.

3. *Ibid.*, p. 14.

4. Niels Henry Sonne, *Liberal Kentucky, 1780 to 1828* (New York: Columbia University Press, 1839). Cf. Eaton, *The Freedom of Thought Struggle*, p. 17.

5. Albert Post, *Popular Freethought in America, 1825–1850* (Columbia University Press, 1943), p. 46.

6. Benjamin M. Palmer, *The Life and Letters of James Henley Thornwell* (Richmond: Whittet and Shepperson, 1875), p. 61.

7. N. L. Rice, *The Signs of the Times* (St. Louis: Keith and Woods, 1855), p. 106. Cf. A. C. Dayton, "The Bible and Spirit Rappings," *Southern Baptist Review and Eclectic*, Vol. I (1855), pp. 110–126, 276–288, 413–425, 515–530.

8. Olim, "Religion in Colleges," *Evangelical and Literary Magazine*, Vol. XI (1828), pp. 505–506.

9. Orval Filbeck, "The Christian Evidence Movement in American Schools" (Ph.D. dissertation, University of Texas, 1944).

10. Kenneth Ballard Murdock, *Increase Mather, the Foremost American Puritan* (Harvard University Press, 1925), p. 163.

11. *Ibid.*, p. 164.

12. Charles E. Cuningham, *Timothy Dwight, 1752–1817, a Biography* (The Macmillan Company, 1942), p. 160.

13. Thomas L. Nichols, *Forty Years in America* (London: John Maxwell and Co., 1864), Vol. I, p. 76.

14. Cf. Crockett, *Autobiography*, p. 248.

15. Nichols, *Forty Years in America*, Vol. I, p. 76.

16. *Ibid.*, p. 77.

Chapter 7

MODERN SURVIVALS OF THE CAMP MEETING

1. Charles Drake, *Pioneer Life in Kentucky*, pp. 191–193.

2. William G. McLoughlin, Jr., *Modern Revivalism*, p. 391.

3. Oren Arnold, "Riding the Gospel Circuit," *Pageant*,

August–September, 1945, pp. 97–100.
4. See *Newsweek*, July 20, 1970, pp. 50–55.
5. See *Newsweek*, May 1, 1950, pp. 66–67.
6. Cf. *Life*, July 1, 1957, p. 92.
7. *Newsweek*, July 20, 1970, p. 54.
8. "Racism Saddens Graham," *The Houston Post*, June 4, 1970, Sec. 1.
9. Harold H. Martin, "Billy Graham," *The Saturday Evening Post*, April 13, 1963, p. 18.
10. Sid Moody, "Evangelist in the Bible-Belt," *The Atlanta Journal and Constitution*, Sept. 4, 1966, p. 36.
11. H. L. Mencken, *A Mencken Chrestomathy* (Alfred A. Knopf, Inc., 1949), pp. 392–398.

Chapter 8

SENSATIONALISM AND EXCESSES

1. John A. Womeldorf, "Rattlesnake Religion," *The Christian Century*, Vol. LXIV, Dec. 10, 1947, pp. 1517–1518.
2. Lester Kinsolving, "Dazzling Successor to Sister Aimee," *Spotlight, The Houston Post*, July 5, 1970.
3. Hayes B. Jacobs, "High Priest of Faith Healing," *Harper's Magazine*, Vol. CCXXIV, February 1962, pp. 39–40.
4. *Ibid.*
5. Cf. *ibid.*, p. 40.
6. *Ibid.*, p. 41.
7. W. E. Mann, "What About Oral Roberts?" *The Christian Century*, Vol. LXXIII (May 1956), p. 1018.
8. Cf. Phil Dessauer, "God Heals—I Don't," *Coronet*, Vol. XXXVIII, October 1955, p. 60.
9. *Ibid.*, p. 58.
10. *Ibid.*
11. John Kobler, "Oral Roberts, King of the Faith Healers," *American Magazine*, Vol. CLXI, May 1956, p. 88.
12. Jacobs, *loc. cit.*, p. 41.
13. Dessauer, *loc. cit.*, p. 58.
14. Kobler, *loc. cit.*, p. 88.
15. *Ibid.*
16. Mann, *loc. cit.*, p. 1018
17. Dessauer, *loc. cit.*, p. 52.

18. *Ibid.*, p. 54.

19. Kobler, *loc. cit.*, p. 90.

20. William Hedgepeth, "Brother A. A. Allen on the Gospel Trail: He Heals, He Heals, and He Turns You On with God," *Look*, Vol. XXXIII, No. 20 (October 7, 1969), p. 30.

21. Cf. Hedgepeth, *loc. cit.*, p. 29. Also see *Miracle Magazine*, May 1969 to December 1969, for background information.

22. Hedgepeth, *loc. cit.*, p. 28.

23. *Ibid.*, p. 29.

24. *Ibid.*

25. Since only the type of behavior is of interest because it relates to that which occurred in the first half of the nineteenth century (and later, if one wishes to labor the point), the names are withheld.

26. *Miracle Magazine*, Vol. XIV, June 1969, p. 15.

27. *Ibid.*

28. *Ibid.* Vol. XIV, July 1969, p. 2.

29. *Ibid.*, Vol. XIV, September 1969, pp. 4–5.

30. *Ibid.* Vol. XIV, August 1969, p. 5.

31. *Ibid.*, Vol. XIV, December 1969, p. 16.

32. *Ibid.*, p. 11.

33. *Ibid.*

34. Reported by Ralph Dighton in *Birmingham News-Age Herald*, Feb. 15, 1948, Sec. A, p. 19.

35. Hal Wingo, "The Confessions of Marjoe," *Life*, Sept. 8, 1972, p. 60.

36. *Ibid.*

37. *Ibid.*

38. Cf. *Playboy*, September 1972, pp. 31–32.

39. Charlene Warnken, "A Young Evangelist Denounces Marjoe's Expose of Evangelism," *The Houston Post*, Sept. 16, 1972, Sec. AA, p. 16.

40. Cf. *Life*, June 30, 1972, pp. 44–45.

41. *Ibid.*, p. 43.

42. Edward B. Fiske, "The Jesus People," *International Herald Tribune*, July 5, 1971, p. 14.

43. William C. Martin, "The God Huckster of Radio," *The Atlantic*, June 1970, pp. 51–56.

44. *Ibid.*, p. 52.

45. *Ibid.*
46. *Ibid.*, pp. 53–54.
47. *Ibid.*, p. 54.
48. Aldous Huxley, *Brave New World Revisited* (Harper & Brothers, 1958), pp. 52–53.

Chapter 9

EMOTIONALISM IN EDUCATION AND POLITICS

1. Kenneth K. Bailey, *Southern White Protestantism in the Twentieth Century* (Harper & Brothers, 1964), p. 29.
2. *The Houston Post*, Feb. 24, 1959, Sec. 1, p. 6.
3. Bailey, *Southern White Protestantism*, pp. 35–36.
4. *Ibid.*, p. 47.
5. *Ibid.*, p. 46.
6. The law was repealed on November 1, 1969.
7. Bailey, *Southern White Protestantism*, p. 78.
8. *Ibid.*, p. 90.
9. *The Houston Post*, April 15, 1967, Sec. 2, p. 8.
10. Bailey, *Southern White Protestantism*, p. 105.
11. Miriam Kass, "Inside on Evolution," *Perspective, The Houston Post*, Oct. 11, 1964, p. 7.
12. Gayle McNutt, *The Houston Post*, Nov. 10, 1964, Sec. 1, p. 6; cf. *ibid.*, Oct. 15, 1964, Sec. 1, p. 15; Oct. 17, 1964, Sec. 1, p. 8. Also Blair Justice, *The Houston Post*, Oct. 11, 1964, Sec. 1, p. 1.
13. *The Houston Post*, Nov. 24, 1952, Sec. 1, p. 1.
14. Charlene Warnken, "Pearland Baptists Begin 'Bibliothon,' " *The Houston Post*, Oct. 6, 1972, Sec. A, p. 12.

Chapter 10

REFLECTIONS ON THE BIBLE BELT MYSTIQUE

1. Walter Hines Page, "The Forgotten Man," in Richmond Croom Beatty *et al.* (eds.), *The Literature of the South* (Scott, Foresman and Company, 1952), pp. 495–506. (From *The Rebuilding of Old Commonwealths*, by Walter Hines Page [Houghton Mifflin Company, 1905].)
2. Marshall Frady, "God and Man in the South," *The Atlantic Monthly*, Vol. CXIX (January 1967), p. 40.

3. *Ibid.*

4. James McBride Dabbs, *Who Speaks for the South?* (Funk & Wagnalls, 1967), p. 103.

5. Allen F. Stein and Thomas N. Walters, *The Southern Experience in Short Fiction* (Scott, Foresman & Company, 1971), p. 1.

6. John William Corrington and Miller Williams (eds.), *Southern Writing in the Sixties/Fiction* (Louisiana State University Press, 1966), pp. lx-x.

7. Dabbs, *Who Speaks for the South?* p. 254.

8. *Ibid.*

9. Cf. C. Vann Woodward, *The Burden of Southern History* (Louisiana State University Press, 1968), pp. 16–25.

10. Dabbs, *Who Speaks for the South?* p. 281.

11. See *ibid.*, p. 259.

12. Willie Morris, *North Toward Home* (Houghton Mifflin Company, 1967), p. 46.

13. *Ibid.*, pp. 38–39.